T0077807

Forever YOU

*Empower Your Life by Reconnecting
with Your Spiritual Path*

MARII K. K. ZIERHUT

BALBOA.
PRESS
A DIVISION OF HAY HOUSE

Balboa Press books may be ordered through booksellers or by contacting:

Balboa Press
A Division of Hay House
1663 Liberty Drive
Bloomington, IN 47403
www.balboapress.com
1 (877) 407-4847

Because of the dynamic nature of the Internet, any web addresses or links contained in this book may have changed since publication and may no longer be valid. The views expressed in this work are solely those of the author and do not necessarily reflect the views of the publisher, and the publisher hereby disclaims any responsibility for them.

The author of this book does not dispense medical advice or prescribe the use of any technique as a form of treatment for physical, emotional, or medical problems without the advice of a physician, either directly or indirectly. The intent of the author is only to offer information of a general nature to help you in your quest for emotional and spiritual well-being. In the event you use any of the information in this book for yourself, which is your constitutional right, the author and the publisher assume no responsibility for your actions.

Any people depicted in stock imagery provided by Thinkstock are models, and such images are being used for illustrative purposes only. Certain stock imagery © Thinkstock.

Printed in the United States of America.

ISBN: 978-1-4525-9204-6 (sc)
ISBN: 978-1-4525-9205-3 (e)

Balboa Press rev. date: 3/3/2014

In the face of eternity we are
forever young.

Marii at Esna Temple, Egypt (2011)

This book is dedicated to you

Table of Contents

Introduction

Forever You is about reaching a point in life where you choose happiness and healing, no matter what the circumstances in your life may be right now.

I hope that I will be able to help you make a conscious decision to enjoy life henceforth, to know what it's like to enjoy living on this planet, as this body, at this time, in your surroundings, whatever the challenges may be.

My message is a message of faith, courage, patience, gratitude, love and compassion.

I hope that you who are reading this have dreams. Dreams you have yet to fulfill, goals you have yet to accomplish.

By reading *Forever You*, I hope that you will gain assurance that you have those dreams and goals for a reason and that you are not alone, not for one second of your life. I encourage you to start listening to your spiritual glam squad, your loving entourage of angels and spirit guides who magically and lovingly will guide, lead, and comfort you whenever necessary.

Don't think for one minute that your life is a failure; it is a success, simply because you are here.

Your Soul has embarked on an adventurous experience on this planet because you – being that Soul - want to evolve, grow and learn.

Develop depth and faith in your own abilities, your own strength and give thanks to God.
Lead by example, inspire, participate, help, and communicate. Share your stories. Develop a sense of humour.

Keep moving on. You can do it.

- Be grateful for what you've got.

- Do good and be kind to others. Help whenever you can but don't let anyone use you.

- Leave room for the miraculous, the inexplicable, the fantastic, the mysterious, as not everything can be explained by reason.

- Work hard, stay humble and ask life to help you reach the goals rooted in your heart.

There is, however, much more to it!

In the face of eternity we are *forever*. We always will be, we always have been, and we ARE now. We are forever learning and evolving.

Knowing this and living your life accordingly, you will feel and attract more and more joy into your life.

Being forever means the following on a conscious or unconscious level:

- Loving yourself, life, and others

- Growing from adversity, pain and suffering

- Being vulnerable and strong

- Being grounded, yet connected to the Spiritual

- Developing gratitude, positivity, hope, and faith

My aim is to lead you towards painting a beautiful picture of your present, full of gratitude and peace. May you understand and know that this road you're walking is the road that may lead you to your dreams. All you need to do is keep on walking.

I cannot promise you that your life will ever be perfect or that you will indeed achieve your dreams in the way you are imagining. And even if a particular dream does become reality, will there be other obstacles in the way? No-one can know that. However, I believe that life and any burden we need to bear may become easier, if we know and acknowledge that we are watched over by dear old friends in the spirit world who love us unconditionally.

This book may, at times, seem negative. It may seem that I am focusing and talking about the negative quite a bit. The reason for that is that I don't believe anybody's life is a walk in the park. We come here to learn, to evolve as Souls in time and space. If life were an easy road, it would be called "Easy Road" but it's called life. In everybody's life there will be challenges and difficult situations, suffering and conflict because that is a way to gain depth. It helps us to connect with and relate to others truly and completely. Therefore I say, feel the pain, feel the desperation, and then pull yourself out of it, grow from it, develop an attitude of gratitude and live with the deep conviction that, no matter what the situation, you can make a conscious choice to see the good and to focus on the positive, for this is the only chance you have of true happiness.

As a Soul you are forever *young* – you never grow older, only wiser!

In a nutshell, you are *forever*.

You are forever *you*.

The Road goes ever on and on.

(J.R.R. Tolkien, The Lord of the Rings)

chapter 1

About You

"Let us so live that when we come to die even the undertaker will be sorry." (Mark Twain)

"Good actions give strength to ourselves and inspire good actions in others." (Plato)

"Love is what we were born with. Fear is what we learn. The spiritual journey is the unlearning of fear and prejudices and the acceptance of love back into our hearts. Love is the essential reality and our purpose on earth. To be consciously aware of it, to experience love in ourselves and others, is the meaning of life. Meaning does not lie in things. Meaning lies in us."
(Marianne Williamson)

"We are made of dreams and bones."
(Peter, Paul & Mary, Garden Song)

"Only God knows where the story ends for me. But I know where the story begins."
(Mary J. Blige, No More Drama)

* * *

Who are you? Who are you? Who are you really deep down? Who are you? Which three words describe you? Who are you? Who are you?

Ask yourself this question many times in a row and you will find that you get confused and don't know anything any more. Do you sometimes wake up wondering whether this life is real or just an illusion? "There is no spoon", Neo said in *The Matrix*. Is there a YOU, really? Why are you here? Is this really happening?

We tend to get so busy, so tangled up in everyday life that we never seem to pause to think and feel what the meaning is of our lives. We carry on, tired, stressed, worried (all too often) and never have a minute to ourselves to connect with the Core of our Being. Thus, we forget that this planet is not our True Home, which makes it even more important to enjoy the time spent here. It is like going on a holiday and not enjoying a minute of it – what's the point? We must make time for ourselves at least once a day to be alone with ourselves, to feel who we are and to reconnect to our purpose here on Earth.

If you are single, or you have time to yourself to be solitary each day, this may be a challenge, not just a blessing. Many people can't be still with themselves, they always need to do something, and they need to occupy themselves. Why? It takes courage and depth to spend time alone with the person you are, as this requires you to *like* the person you are. You have to really enjoy your own company and to value and love yourself.

Society does not like singles, really. There is this expectation that everyone must be in a relationship, a marriage best of all, and if people choose to be alone or happen to be so there must be something wrong with them! Naturally, I could not disagree more. I would much rather be single than stuck in a relationship with someone who makes my life more difficult by being temperamental, rude, selfish or insensitive!

Having the courage to be on your own also means that you are developing some independence, knowing that you do not need anyone by your side. From that may come the wish to have someone to share your life with, but not the necessity.

I firmly believe that there are certain things you learn about yourself in a relationship, there are equally as many things you learn about yourself whilst being on your own.

A few minutes of seclusion a day, a few minutes of breathing in silence and letting the thoughts just drift, will do the trick. You will be reminded that there is a greater purpose to your life than just your earthly existence.

Ask yourself "Who am I?" and then meditate on the answer for a few minutes – which adjectives best describe you?

Take some time out for yourself each day to reflect and dream.

❖ Who are you?

"Be yourself. Everyone else is already taken."
(Oscar Wilde)

* * *

Let's do a short exercise someone once taught me:

Think of three animals and their characteristics. Write them down here:

Animal 1 and its characteristics	
Animal 2 and its characteristics	
Animal 3 and its characteristics	

Animal 1 is how you see yourself, Animal 2 is how others see you, and Animal 3 is who you really are.

How do you feel about the results? Do you recognise yourself?

Another way to define yourself is by symbolism - If you were a colour, what colour would you be?

If you were a ..., what ... would you be?

Complete the following sentences:

- If I were a house, I'd be a _____

- If I were a car, I'd be a _____

- If I were a tree, I'd be a _____

- If I were a mountain, I'd be _____

- If I were a river, I'd be _____

- If I were an island, I'd be _____

- If I were a piece of classical music, I'd be

  _____

- If I were an instrument, I'd be a _____

- If I were a song, I'd be _____

- If I were a film, I'd be _____

- If I were a _____, I'd be

  _____

What does that tell you about you? Have fun reflecting! Enjoy putting information together that sums up your beliefs, feelings, and thoughts.

If you have ever watched "Inside the Actor's Studio"[1], you will have come across the Pivot questionnaire. James Lipton asks famous actors and actresses questions about their strongest likes and dislikes in life, e.g. words, sounds, career paths, inspirations etc. This is another good way to find out about who you are as a person now.

He also asks them the following question:

If Heaven exists, what would you like to hear God say when you arrive at the Pearly Gates?

By focusing on the core of your being, you forget, for one moment, all the adversity around you, all your challenges, all your worries, and you return to who you really are, deep inside, a unique wonderful perfect diamond of a person.

Reconnect with your uniqueness and be proud of it! No-one in the world is like you, feels like you, looks or speaks like you!

> You are unique. No-one in the world is like you.

❖ Your name

"The sweetest sound to any person in any language is the sound of their own name." (Mark Twain)

* * *

---

1   http://www.wowzone.com/pivot.htm

Your name is the essence of you, it represents your persona to yourself and to the outside world. It is your ticket to ride in this life.

Some people have nicknames, but when they introduce themselves to someone new, they may choose to use their official name.

Some people even have more than one nickname, a family nickname and/or a nickname used by their friends.

Try to use other people's names in conversations whenever you can. This will immediately create a bond between the two of you.

In *Mutant Message Down Under* Marlo Morgan[2]writes about the Aborigines in Australia:

"Each child is named at birth, but it is understood that as a person develops, the birth name will be outgrown, and the individuals will select for themselves a more appropriate greeting. Hopefully, one's name will change several times in a lifetime as wisdom, creativity, and purpose also become more clearly defined with time."

I love the idea that a person can change their name, just like a snake sheds its skin from time to time. Changing one's name officially can be quite costly, but why not change your name from time to time to symbolise our spiritual growth as well as our willingness to reinvent yourself for the better?

---

2   Marlo Morgan *Mutant Message Down Under*, p. 46

Maybe you never even liked your birth name in the first place? Play with your possibilities and have fun!

When I moved from Austria to England in 2001 my life changed in many ways. I was living and working in a foreign country, which I thoroughly enjoyed. Sadly, however, many of my closest Austrian friends suddenly and inexplicably turned against me, making up stories about me that were untrue and revealing themselves as uncaring and cold individuals. As my old life was falling apart, I decided it was time to embrace my new life. One way in which I did this was by changing my first name from Maria to Mary. I had always loved the name Mary, plus I discovered that the name Mary perfectly matched my date of birth in numerological terms. So I asked everyone, my family included, to start calling me "Mary". My family and (remaining) friends agreed to do so. I am particularly grateful to my parents for making this transition easy for me. I believe that my parents' souls and me as the new soul joining them in this earthly life had picked my name in unison originally, but in 2001 it was time for me to start a new phase in my life with a new name. I love the name Mary, and I have become completely used to it, I do not even turn around when I hear someone call the name "Maria".

Since 2001 I have changed my name three times, but only slightly. I did this at times in my life when I felt I had, as Marlo Morgan describes it, "outgrown" my old Self and entered a new phase.

I added Kaona Kanaloa to my name in 2005 to express my spiritual connection with Hawaii. Kaona means "double meaning", and "Kanaloa", aside of being one of the major Hawaiian Gods of Creation and the Ocean, means "the great calm/stillness."

In 2012 I changed the spelling of Mary to Marii, simply because it looks fresher and more exciting to me.

Only recently did I decide to change "Kaona" to "Kaiona", meaning "beautiful ocean" as well as the Hawaiian Goddess of Mount Ka'ala who protects all those who are lost.

Allow yourself to embrace new aspects of your identity as you grow in life.

Adapt your name to reflect a major shift.

❖ Your contribution to the world

"If you think you are too small to make a difference, try sleeping with a mosquito." (Dalai Lama)

* * *

In what way are you contributing to the world around you? Are you an active member of your community? Do you give time or money to charity?

Try to give, to be kind and patient to others to the best of your ability. One kind word may stay with a stranger forever.

Collect "proof" of your contributions to other people's lives. Keep Thank You cards, make notes of special conversations you had with people where you believe you influenced their life in a positive way. In the same way, thank others when they are kind to you.

As human beings we want to belong, and we want to feel that our existence has a meaning.

Being a teacher, I am lucky to have received many wonderful letters from students and parents over the years. I have a special folder where I collect such treasured keepsakes of mine. When I am feeling low, I read and re-read the letters, cards and emails. This helps me remember that I can have a positive impact on others.

Be kind to others in deeds and words.

Try to remember times when you took the opportunity to help others, as this will make you feel better about your place in this world.

❖ Heroes and heroines

If you could have dinner with two celebrities, dead or alive, who would you choose and why? What are the qualities you admire about them? What would you ask them?

Celebritiy 1 and why?

Celebrity 2 and why?

What if I told you that you *are* actually like them, or you would not have chosen them? You share important core qualities with these people, or you would not feel drawn towards them.

You can only see in others what you are yourself. Other people are a mirror to you. You may not know that you possess those qualities or you may not have had the courage to admit it yet, but let me tell you that you only like things and people that are, mostly, like you.

Just like you buy clothes, furniture, accessories, that are "so you", you can only see in others what is you. Sometimes you like it, sometimes you get annoyed by it, and sometimes you are even scared of it. Some people may scare you because you are afraid of your own light, your own strength. Some people may annoy you because they show you the exact qualities you possess and which annoy you about yourself.

Therefore, it is a good idea to choose people who inspire you in your life as role models. People you look up to, perhaps even celebrities that embody a part of yourself that you want to expand on, to improve on. Put a picture of them up by your bed, so to remind yourself every single day where your motivation to achieve and to grow comes from. These people will also give you strength, as they embody part of you. If they can do it, you can do it!

Some of my "celebrity icons" have been James Cook, the noble explorer and cartographer, Madonna, the fearless and progressive feminist, Marilyn Monroe, the eternal beauty, Groucho Marx, the unforgettable comedian bringing so much laughter to the world, and last but not least Céline Dion, the lady with the big heart and the big voice who has experienced adversity in her life and has thrived from it, being all the more loving and caring.

Whoever your heroes or heroines are, make them an inspiration for you on a daily basis.

> Make your heroes and heroines a daily inspiration in your life.

❖ Beauty

"Più bella cosa non c'è di te" ("There is nothing more beautiful than you", Eros Ramazzotti)

"All little girls should be told they're pretty, even if they aren't." (Marilyn Monroe)

"A good heart will help you to a bonny face (...) and a bad one will turn the bonniest into something worse than ugly." (Emily Brontë, Wuthering Heights)

* * *

I cannot remember anyone telling me in my childhood that I was beautiful, unique, wonderful and special. I wish I had been told that and often, for it can make such a difference to one's self esteem. I always felt loved 100% but I never felt pretty.

That is probably why I developed such an extreme sense of vanity from my early 20's onwards. Like many people I am a vain person, I want to be seen as beautiful by the world!

However, outer beauty is just half the deal. I know people who are beautiful on the outside, but they are cold, unfeeling, and selfish, so their beauty starts to fade rather quickly the better you know them.

For many people outer beauty is a core value. They work incessantly and addictively on improving their looks, having more and more surgery. Their self-worth is completely tied up in their outer beauty.

The opposite is true of other people. Inner beauty shines even brighter and brings much more joy and happiness to the beholder than outer beauty.

I believe we should all care to nourish both aspects of our beauty. As Souls we are forever beautiful and pure, no matter what happens in our lifetime on Earth, our Soul is lightful and good and cannot be destroyed by anything we do or experience.

A healthy sense of vanity is good for one's confidence, but true beauty shines from within, through good deeds, sensitivity, generosity, depth, unconditional love, humility and faith.

Treasure your body and your Soul. You have chosen this body in this lifetime, you predetermined for a reason what colour of skin/hair/eyes you would have, how tall or short, corpulent or thin you would be, and where your physical weaknesses lie.

True beauty shines from within and complements outer beauty.

Work on both.

❖ Confidence and self-worth

"As soon as you trust yourself, you will know how to live." (Johann Wolfgang von Goethe, *Faust*)

* * *

Confidence and true self-worth based on love and appreciation for the person you are and have become through learning cannot be bought or expressed by things, such as certificates, diplomas, possessions, or indeed one's hierarchical position in a company or one's bank balance.

If you do not feel worthy of your place in this world, if you do not love and respect yourself, truly and deeply, *no thing* can make you do this. The only *person* who can, is you! Therefore nurture and value the unique connection you have with yourself as much as you can.

This does not imply taking an attitude of selfishness, egotism and narcissism.

True confidence should be based on inner, not outer values.

Ask yourself:

Why am I unique and wonderful?

Why am I beautiful?

Why do I love myself?

The answer to these questions is simply – because I am!

If the answer to any of these questions is something along the lines of "because I have a good job, because I earn lots of money, because I just graduated from uni with honours, because I just lost some weight, because I won a Beauty contest, because I was the guest of honour at a dinner last week ...", you are basing your self-worth on outer values, when there is so much more to you than that!!!

Work on focusing on inner values instead.
Confidence based on the deep conviction that you are a worthy human being equal to all others is true confidence.

Confidence based on outer values, such as holding a high position in a business, is closely connected with the idea of power. If you have inferiors, you have certain rights. Those rights may include giving open criticism, making decisions others disagree with, giving orders, or even firing people. No matter what your rights are, always remember that on a human level everyone is your equal. The least you can do is be fair and civil and not abuse the power invested in you by outer institutions.

When I was working as a teacher a colleague who was in a higher position than me used my classroom one day. Without notifying me, he had all the tables moved out (and not back in afterwards), made a mess of the room and opened up my cupboard to take out my felt-tips and other creative resources to use in the lesson with his students. When I asked him to let me know in advance next time he would be using my room and not to use my materials, he aggressively told me that the materials belonged to the school and that "my" room was simply a classroom to be used by whoever needed it.

He clearly felt he had the right to invade and vandalise my work space as well as take resources bought by me. This is a typical example of someone abusing their power. On paper, he did have the right to do what he did because he had power over me and I had to accept his actions no matter what. However, on a human level he failed to treat me with respect. His confidence and self-worth were clearly tied to his position in the school and he forgot that he was just another human being like me.

True confidence shines from within with love and kindness and respect for others - it is not based on one's hierarchical position at work or diplomas acquired over the years.

chapter 2

About Happiness

"What a splendid day! Isn't it good just to be alive on a day like this? I pity the people who aren't born yet for missing it. They may have good days, of course, but they can never have this one."
(L.M. Montgomery, Anne of Green Gables)

"I, not events, have the power to make me happy or unhappy today. I can choose which it shall be. Yesterday is dead, tomorrow hasn't arrived yet. I have just one day, today, and I'm going to be happy in it." (Groucho Marx)

"Our greatest glory is not in never falling, but in getting up every time we do." (Confucius)

"If you would be a real seeker after truth, it is necessary that at least once in your life you doubt, as far as possible, all things." (René Descartes)

> *"That place... is strong with the dark side of the Force. A domain of evil it is. In you must go."*

"What's in there?"
"Only what you take with you."

(Yoda and Luke Skywalker, The Empire Strikes Back)

"Happiness is not something ready made. It comes from our own actions." (Dalai Lama)

"In every life, no matter how full or empty one's purse, there is tragedy. It is the one promise life always fulfills. Thus, happiness is a gift. And the trick is not to expect it, but to delight in it when it comes, and to add to other people's store of it."
(Charles Dickens, Nicholas Nickleby)

* * *

I do not believe in reading self-help books that tell you to push away all negative thoughts and feelings of inadequacy and replace them with positive thoughts and affirmations. Negative thoughts should never be replaced with positive ones, instead they should be transformed into positive ones. Affirmations are a good tool to use to help with that.

Furthermore, I don't believe that we attract what we *deserve*, I believe rather that we attract what we have *decided* to attract before we came here. We may be able to change the intensity of an experience by prayer and fast-track learning, but we cannot completely avoid an important learning point that we felt on the Other Side we should challenge ourselves with whilst here.

So what should we do when going through a desert period, a time in our lives where nothing seems to go right, one disaster and bad piece of news follows another and we are so depressed that we wonder why we are here and whether this lifetime isn't just a "waste of time"?

What I suggest you do when things are bad, is feel the fear, the anxiety, the desperation, the helplessness to its maximum. Cry, scream, if you want to. Feel as bad as you can, question everything, even your own existence, but ... NEVER lose faith! Let me tell you – there is a purpose to your life, you are here for a valid reason and you deserve to be happy! You deserve to get out of this desert period, step right into an oasis, full of water, palm-trees, flowers, life, beauty and new creations.

And believe me – you will get out! It is a natural phenomenon that downs are followed by ups, the natural flow of things is ups and downs, winter and summer, valley and mountain-top, darkness and light! All extremes do contain within them their opposites.

Therefore, I suggest that you get help if you can – homeopathy is a wonderful way to build your energy up – friends or family you can talk to and trust, - or maybe a doctor? Use all means available to you to pull yourself out of a dark place.

See adversity as a seed and grow from it. Develop depth and compassion along the way.

Difficult times make you stronger as a person; they teach you about sensitivity, compassion, and vulnerability and help you to develop depth and integrity, which will ultimately help you to connect with others and yourself on a deeper level.

If you are artistically inclined, write about your feelings, sing, draw, paint. Use colours and shapes to express how you are feeling. Know that it will get better. By all means, use positive affirmations and thoughts to help, but do not push away the negative feelings totally, for they cannot be replaced. Little by little, you will notice that the negativity will vanish and as positive thoughts push their way through more and more, you will come out of the dark place. You have faced yourself, your darkest thoughts and feelings and you've come out of it alive, well and much more appreciative of yourself and your surroundings. – Just like Luke Skywalker in the cave scene in *The Empire Strikes Back*.

Although life may be here to try you, it will ultimately not fail you.

Develop faith. Believe in the miraculous, the fantastic, the inexplicable, the mysterious. Know that you matter, no matter how small you may be, you are powerful enough to make a difference in the world. Know that there is a purpose to your existence and that you are never alone. Angels and other spirit helpers are with you, especially when you are feeling low, and they will do all they can to get you to obtain a happier state of mind. You may feel their presence, you may not. But know that they are there!

Make a conscious choice that, no matter what the circumstances, you want to enjoy life; you want to know what it is like to be happy *now*. Only you can pull yourself out of this crisis, no-one can do it for you. You are your only hope.

From seeds sown in a crisis, beautiful flowers will grow, you will grow and you will be a beautiful garden admired and loved for its beauty, uniqueness, and strength.

If you push your feelings away and refuse to confront them, the seed that is the crisis may not grow into a flower. It may continue sitting in the mud without coming to the surface. Your garden might continue to look bare. Once you have learnt to surround yourself with the beauty that you are – complete with all your emotions and feelings - you are surrounded by love and beauty wherever you go because you understand that you are that love and beauty on your path. Thus, you have created a scenario of self-love and respect for your soul's earning whilst accepting that the learning is necessary to grow in the first place.

Try to the best of your ability to develop a feeling of happiness NOW. In your darkest moment, think of something you are grateful for *right now*, and pull yourself up bit by bit. Be gentle with yourself.

When we feel down, we often tend to talk to ourselves in a negative way, saying things like "You're no good, no wonder X left you, you are ugly, you don't deserve to be happy." Avoid harsh words to the best of your ability. You would not talk like that to someone you love, so why speak to yourself like that? Instead, build yourself up, tell yourself you are special and beautiful and you deserve better. You are worth it.

Ask your angels to send you healing energy and remember to exhale consciously. Breathe in golden light, bathe in it. Breathe out all darkness. Faith always helps, I have found. It adds hope to the suffering.

Above all, remember that, ultimately, happiness always happens in the now. It won't happen in the future when you've completed a training or met Mr Right or got rid of a health problem. – Yes, these things will have a positive effect on your life, no doubt, but once you have got them in your life, what if you cannot be happy in the now that is then? What if you will keep thinking of things that could go wrong then? You will never reach a state of happiness.

It is your right to feel happy now, right now, at this moment. Don't procrastinate happiness. Now is as good a time as ever to be happy.

Pull yourself out of a dark place by confronting your feelings and fears to the maximum whilst developing a sense of gratitude for the good things you have in your life *right now*.

Acknowledge that no matter how small you may seem you are a powerful being who deserves to experience happiness.

Don't procrastinate – feel happy right now. Any moment in the future is just another now that has yet to happen. If you can feel happy at this minute, you can feel happy at any minute.

You are your only hope for happiness. You will be (with) yourself until the day you die (and beyond), so you might as well learn to *like* yourself, even to *love* yourself, and to develop the skills you need to build yourself up when times are bad.

Ask the angels to send you healing energy. Breathe in golden light, exhale all negativity.

Here is one of my favourite quotes that sums up why happiness has to happen in the present moment. Ultimately, there may never be a future one. No-one can say with 100% certainty that they won't die tonight. Therefore, put the focus in the now.

"It was a brilliant, starry night. There was no moon and I have never seen the starts shine brighter; they appeared to stand right out of the sky, sparkling like cut diamonds. A very light haze, hardly noticeable, hung low over the water ... I have never seen the sea smoother than it was that night; it was like a millpond, and just as innocent looking ... It was the kind of night that made one feel glad to be alive." (Jack Thayer, survivor of the Titanic, on the night of the disaster[3])

> Appreciate the moment.

---

3   Andrew Wilson *Shadow of the Titanic*, p. 25

———— 🐚 ————

chapter 3

About Relationships

"If faut exiger de chacun ce que chacun peut donner."
("You have to demand of everyone what they are capable of giving." Antoine de Saint-Exupéry, The Little Prince)

"No man is an island", said John Donne. I feel we are all islands – in a common sea. We are all, in the last analysis, alone."
(Anne Morrow Lindbergh, Gift from the Sea)

"Love me when I least deserve it, because that's when I really need it." (Swedish proverb)

* * *

Relationships teach us how we deal with others, how we see and treat ourselves, and about being able to learn to love, value, accept ourselves and them for who they are without judging.

Generally speaking, there are five kinds of relationships:

- Family relationships

- Friendships

- Romantic relationships

- Work relationships

- The relationship you have with yourself

I believe that no relationships are random. We charted all influences and connections before we came here, so that we would be pushed, supported, loved, challenged, and healed.

At different stages in life, we may look for different things in relationships. As and if we do grow and evolve, our spiritual and emotional needs and availability to others may vary.

❖ Family relationships

"Family is not an important thing. It's everything." (Michael J. Fox)

"My family is my strength and my weakness." (Aishwarya Rai)

* * *

We often hear "You can choose your friends, but you can't choose your family." This is, of course, not true. We do choose our family; we do choose our parents, our brothers and sisters, our grandparents, our geographical location, our financial and social standing and other circumstances before we incarnate.

Just because we have chosen certain people beforehand does not mean, however, that we are bound to them for life.

As a baby, you are completely dependent on the people around you, usually your mother and father. You depend on them to look after your basic needs like shelter and food. They have complete power over you. Therefore, it is only logical that you must choose this unique relationship you have with the first souls you come into contact with when incarnating. All that derives from this relationship, be it positive, negative or a mixture, is your first learning experience in a new body.

Many of us will experience family as a complex unit, some members of our family push our buttons more than others, and with some we may have a stronger bond of love than with others.

When you look at any family's history or present, I defy you not to uncover any neurotic or irrational patterns, as no family is ever "normal" or "perfect". And any family where people allegedly "get on so well all the time" is a fantasy.

Ideally, a family unit should be a platform where we do not have to pretend to be someone else, where we can be who we are, we can be honest, dishonest, loving, mean, sensible, irrational, clever, stupid, rebellious, and we know we will be loved (unconditionally) no matter what.

As one's family is the first group of people we know when we incarnate, our bond with them is strong and they provide us with our first learning experiences and memories. We share their looks, their genes, their family history. Families provide infinite grounds for conflict and learning, and as such are vital to our spiritual growth and the development of your unique personality and emotional make-up.

Some families are closer than others, but every family, being a unit of souls, will experience problems and spiritual challenges.

Families, being complex units of evolving souls, can and will transform over time. They may also grow by bringing in new souls (children) or by adding a partner's or spouse's family to one's own.

Over the years, there may be fallings-out as well as reconciliations.

When my grandmother Dorothea, my mother's mother, died in 1994, I hardly ever saw my two aunts. I had virtually no relationship with them, they knew very little about me, and I knew very little about them. After my grandmother's death my mother and her sisters had many arguments. There was much unsolved pent-up conflict to work through, as is often the case when someone dies.

After a strong argument between my mother and her sisters, my mother started crying because she felt victimised. That was the beginning of the three sisters re-building their relationships with each other and their extended families.

We started to meet up more often as a family, and the painful experience of having lost my grandmother helped us all form a bond and transform our relationships to a new level.

This does not mean that there has never been any conflict since then. Of course there has – we are all individuals with our own strengths and weaknesses and fears and abilities. On the whole, however, there are many occasions where we enjoy spending time together as a family, and I have developed a good relationship with both my aunts, their husbands and my cousin. Who would have thought? We have all changed and grown over the last 20 years.

I encourage everyone to try to mend relationships with family. If you are unsuccessful in doing so, at least you know that you have tried. But if you are successful, you may be greatly rewarded.

If people are maltreated, neglected, or abused, they have the option to cut all ties with their family. In such cases it is advisable to work through all issues with a therapist or counselor.

The secret of a happy family lies in moments of quality time.

Your family provides opportunities for spiritual growth like nothing else.

Families should be a haven of unconditional love and support to all its members.

You are connected to your family by blood but that does not mean you must continue a relationship with them, if such a relationship is only hurtful to you.

Your partner's or spouse's family adds new aspects of learning as well as new possibilities for both families to transform and to heal.

About Ancestors

"If you cannot get rid of the family skeleton, you may as well make it dance." (George Bernard Shaw)

"Every man is a quotation from all his ancestors." (Ralph Waldo Emerson)

"We must strive to become good ancestors." (Ralph Nader)

"There were times, especially when I was traveling for 'Eat, Pray, Love,' when, I swear to God, I would feel this weight of my female ancestors, all those Swedish farmwives from beyond the grave who were like, 'Go! Go to Naples! Eat more pizza! Go to India, ride an elephant! Do it! Swim in the Indian Ocean. Read those books. Learn a language.'" (Elizabeth Gilbert)

* * *

Ancestors are souls who have incarnated before us in our bloodline and therefore give us our genetic features. We may decide to incarnate into the same bloodline for a few incarnations in a row, but as Souls we tend to incarnate wherever our learning can best be accomplished, and that may mean "switching" bloodlines and countries many times. Remember that true connections between souls are based on a bond of love (on the Other Side as well as on Earth), not of blood.

Many cultures teach us to value and even worship our ancestors.

I believe that we have our ancestors' energy within us, and in many cases their emotional, spiritual, or even physical struggles may be reflected in our own lives. In such cases, we have the chance to transform them and bring a new energy and consciousness into the family.

To disentangle deeply rooted family issues psychotherapy, in particular systemic (family) constellations can be useful.

Adopted children take on the ancestry of both families they are connected with, which makes their heritage more complex.

I believe that many family members who have passed over, regardless of whether we remember or have known them or not, watch over us in great love. They protect and help us, so we can experience happiness by fulfilling our destiny.

Knowing one's family roots can be a grounding experience.

Ask the angels to help you transform any negative family patterns that impact on your well-being, should you know of any in your family's past.

Ask for loving guidance from your ancestors.

❖ Friendships

"The proper office of a friend is to side with you when you are in the wrong. Nearly anybody will side with you when you are in the right." (Mark Twain)

"A friend is a second self." (Aristotle)

"We make a living by what we get, we make a life by what we give." (Winston Churchill)

* * *

We form loving bonds with many people over the years, and I believe that those people whose lives we influence in a positive way and who inspire us in turn, can truly be called friends, or fellow souls, saviors, kindred spirits, or even "angels".

Some friendships may always remain superficial; others may gain depth over the years. Friendships like all relationships are dynamic and ever-changing and need to be worked on or even ended when no longer serving a purpose. This can be very hurtful.

We are all individuals with unique life experiences, and it is a true privilege to be able to share certain aspects of life with one another and grow alongside each other.

I spent the first 26 years of my life in Vienna, Austria. From the age of 14 onwards, I pretty much had the same circle of friends, a group of girls/young women I would share a particularly close bond with. We had the same interests and sense of humour, and we went to the same university, knowing the same people and going through more or less the same experiences of uni life. One of those girls was like a sister to me. Her name was Alice. Alice went on family vacations with us, and we would talk on the phone for hours every day, even if we had seen each other that day. We would share our deepest thoughts, hopes, fears and dreams with one another and were inseparable. When I moved to the UK at the age of 26, I naturally assumed that my friendships in Vienna would survive the geographical separation. That, however, turned out not to be the case. Shortly after I had moved abroad, I noticed that Alice was starting to feel more and more distant and she would say things about me and to me that were untrue and/or hurtful, and most of the other girls would side with her. Little by little, all but two of my friendships broke apart. It was one of the most painful experiences of my life, but I knew that those people were not showing me any love (any more), so I had to move on, attracting other souls and experiences on the way.

Friendships like all relationships need to be worked on. If you trust someone and they deliberately hurt you, misuse that trust or even betray you, it is probably best to end the friendship. Learn from it, and move on. In other cases, a friend's actions may be hurtful, but it may be necessary to hear their side of the story. This will give you an opportunity to work through it. Few friendships survive a storm and find gold in its wake. Such friendships are to be valued most highly.

Be a person of depth, not of superficiality

Don't say "We must get together for dinner some time." or "You must come round and meet my family some time.", if you don't really mean it. This will give the other person false hope and a false sense of friendship. It will make you look shallow and unloving. Instead share what you've got with an open heart. Say something like, "I'd love to have you round for dinner some time, but at the moment I'm too busy. How do you feel about the ...?" - Say a date in a month or two if necessary.

Avoid people who only talk about themselves. Listening to a friend is important, but not all the time. Exchanging ideas, viewpoints, stories and relating to one another is key to any good friendship. People who are in love with themselves are not really interested in you.

Don't take it for granted when people are genuinely nice to you. They may pay you a compliment, give you a small present, or write you a lovely card. Some friends may give you their time and support. When this happens, you must at least say thank you for it. Often we get tangled up in everyday life and chaos, and we forget to express our gratitude to those who hold their hands out to us, loving us and giving to us from their hearts. If your life is very hectic, make sure you say thank you and stay in touch when you have got some breathing space again, even if this is month afterwards. Nobody will ever be mad at you for saying a heart-felt thank you to them, even if it is late. They will understand. If you don't say thank you, they might feel hurt and you might lose a loving person as a friend. Someone once told me that a friendship is like a porcelain jewellery box – when it is dropped, it breaks into thousands of pieces and it's irreparable.

No matter how hard you try, if you squeeze oranges, you'll never get apple juice.
Acknowledge that people are what they are, and up to a certain extent they won't change. You are fighting a losing battle if you are waiting for people to change, just so they can fit into your circle of friends. Make sure you surround yourself with people who share your interests, sense of humour, world vision, as well as your moral code.

One of my female relatives has had a friend who tried to seduce every single one of her boyfriends. When I found out about this piece of family gossip, I was shocked and to this day I cannot understand why you would want someone like that with you and around you, let alone why you would call them a "friend". But people *are* different, and for my female relative other things are more important in life plus she finds such behaviour acceptable and/or she knows she can handle it.

Lemon juice for me? No, thank you! I like cherries ...

As a child I used to have very few friends. But the friends I had – though there was only a small number – I really cared about and valued their friendships. I always cared enough to pick my friends carefully, yet I wasn't arrogant, but I knew immediately which souls I wanted to connect with. Sometimes I got it wrong and I picked someone as my friend who disappointed me or hurt me, but I have to say that really did not happen a lot when I was a child. Most of the time I got it right.

The point I'm trying to make here is that my parents and teachers would constantly tell me to surround myself with many friends, not just a few special ones, so life was going to be more fun and I was going to have a better time. That was the wrong thing to say to me and it annoyed me beyond measure! Why should I have friendships with people I don't even like, people who – in my view – were way too superficial to understand or care about my feelings, thoughts and dreams? How would that help my happiness? Why should I do that? Just because they say it? Certainly not! So I stuck with my friendship pattern. I knew from a very young age what I wanted and what was right for me.

Stick with your own beliefs about friendship, regardless of what other people say!

A lot of people are the opposite of me. They enjoy having many friends, whereby the depth of their friendships is not particularly important to them. They just like company. On the whole, I could never follow that friendship pattern. People are different, and it's ok, we just need to be true to ourselves.

Friendships provide wonderful opportunities for growth.

Be grateful for your friends and cherish your friendships.

Eliminate false friends. Don't surround yourself with anyone who makes you feel bad about yourself or is not trustworthy.

❖ Romantic relationships

"I always wished that I could find someone as beautiful as you. (...) But in the process I forgot that I was just as good as you." (Madonna, *X-Static Process*)

"When one is a stranger to oneself then one is estranged from others, too. If one is out of touch with oneself, then one cannot touch others."
(Anne Morrow Lindbergh, Gift from the Sea)

* * *

A happy and loving relationship on a soul level contains not only great love but also the element of freedom within it. Therefore, do not ground yourself through your partner, depending on him/her completely. Instead, the two of you should aim to be like two beautiful, well-rooted trees, growing upwards towards the sky, whilst your roots and branches lovingly touch, support, and encourage one another.

About dating

❖ Ladies out there – let the man take the lead! Men out there – you're the man!
Call me old-fashioned but I do not believe that females who pursue a man will not find happiness with him in the long run. Let a man choose you and then say either yes or no. You can still say no! You have lost nothing. A man needs to be the man! He needs to accept the challenge to fight for a female, and it will be his valued victory. Just listen to happy couples! Almost every happy couple who has stayed together for a long time, the man took the lead in the beginning of their relationship.

❖ Never go out with a married person or someone in a relationship!
Never!!!!!!!!! If they are cheating on someone else with you, one day they'll cheat on you with someone else.

❖ Only date people you like and you want to get to know better. I found this to be the best rule. Friends and family might advise you to just go for it and never say no if someone asks you out. Personally, I feel this is a load of rubbish. Why should I go out with someone just because he asks me? There are many reasons why to go out with someone, but just because they ask you is none of them. I am allowed to say no if I do not want to go out with this person and don't want them to get their hopes up. If I am true to myself, I can say yes or no, depending on how I feel, and I am honest with myself and the other person from the start.
Ladies - if it is meant to be, he will ask you out again and again until you finally say yes happily.
Men – keep asking her out, perseverance usually pays off!

❖ Be who you are. Be you. Do not say what you think your date wants to hear. Do not compromise who you are. Be honest. Be vulnerable. Be you. Remember you're already "married" to yourself and you might consider extending yourself with them!

❖ Try to be a grown-up adult, not a child! Look for a grown-up, not a child to be with!
Here is the difference:

What is the difference between a boy and a man? A girl and a woman?

A BOY ... A GIRL ...	A MAN ... A WOMAN ...
Has no or few principles, does not think about his actions	Has clear principles and acts accordingly
Takes all good things for granted	Feels grateful for the good things in life
Blames other people and avoids responsibility whenever possible	Takes responsibility for his life and his actions and decisions
Clams up when need arises to talk about his feelings and keeps his/her joy and (self-)love to himself /herself	Shares the love and joy he/she feels inside and is courageous enough to also share the pain and sadness
Only shares some aspects of his/her personality	Shares everything with the person he/she loves
Exhibits superficiality and childish behaviour	Exhibits maturity and depth
Thinks short-term	Thinks long-term
Seeks passion and fulfillment only in some aspects of a relationship	Seeks passion and fulfillment on all levels

Displays thrift and fear of losing what he/she has	Displays generosity and knows that he/she can only gain from loving someone with a full heart
Feels sorry for himself/herself and is unable to understand other people's feelings	Has the ability to empathise
Thinks only of himself/herself	Respects himself/herself but thinks of others first
Sees love as a thing	Sees love as a blessing
Uses "I" a lot	Uses "we" a lot, especially when he/she talks about anything connected to the other person/ the relationship
Must control everything and keeps secrets	Is able to trust
Arrogant, ungrateful, selfish	Humble, grateful, considerate

I would like to mention that not all romantic relationships are heterosexual. We are all individuals, and our love patterns are just as unique. Whatever people's sexual preference, the only thing that should matter between two people is the love and appreciation they feel for each other. The purer that bond, the freer it is of any fear, power or control issues, the happier, deeper and stronger the relationship will be.

About love and infatuation

❖ No matter how infatuated you are with someone – alarm bells should go off in your head if your partner is not nice to your family or friends! If someone is not nice to other people, chances are that one day they won't be nice to you. It's only logical that one day you might be a victim of their insensitivity, selfishness or meanness. Why should they spare you?
You should re-think that relationship.

❖ Each person's love strategy is different. Some people are *visual* lovers, they like to give gifts, some are *auditory*, they like to say "I love you", some are *kinesthetic*; they like to hug and touch. Your own love strategy might not match another person's, i.e. you might show a lot of visual love, and get back kinesthetic love. Beware if you do not get anything back at all. I strongly believe giving and receiving should be in balance in every relationship.

Find a partner who matches your interests, sense of humour, values, views and visions for the future.

Stay true to yourself at all times.

Beware when your partner is rude to your family. It is only logical that one day, you might be the victim of their insensitivity and selfishness.

About heartache

Nothing in the world is more painful than heartache.

"I loved you so much and you betrayed me! How could you do that? Am I not good enough? What did I do wrong? What could I have done differently?"

Heartache is like road works obstructing your path. You hope every day that the dust and noise will be gone, but it all lasts a while. One day, suddenly, the road works are gone, there is so much space and traffic moves quicker and freer again. Patience is of the essence in order to deal with heartache. Throwing yourself into the next relationship without a period of reflection and/or mourning may not bring you any learning and you may end up in a similar situation with yet another similarly unreliable, selfish, abusive, unfaithful, or unfeeling partner.

The list of love (Is it always love?) stories is endless. Nearly every one of us has at least one bad one to share. Why is that? Is it because we first need to know what we do not want, so we can move on to what we *do* want? Is it because hurt makes us stronger? Is it because we first make a poor choice of partner because we do not see how much happiness we really deserve? Do we choose a partner who reflects our insecurities back to us, so that when we get our heart broken, we have certain proof that we are not good enough, that we never were, that we never will be. FIDDLESTICKS!!!

Heartache - like all suffering - is and opportunity for you to grow and to connect to your Core. It is a chance for you to seek and find more love and light than ever within yourself and to develop depth of feeling and character.

❖ It is what it is, it ain't what it ain't. Whatever it is, was, it really does not matter. The only thing that matters is that you don't forsake the one *true love* of your life – you.

No matter how hard you try, you can never run away from the person YOU are. In other words - you are unable to ever break up with you. Acknowledge your uniqueness, wonderful-ness and loveable-ness, no matter what. Don't ever believe you have to be perfect to be loved, perfect people are boring. Love yourself for your flaws, as well as your strengths, and see both with an unconditionally loving heart, the same heart you use to love your sweetheart with. See yourself as you see the person you love most, and you will automatically cease being hard on yourself and blaming yourself for your past. Bless your past. Without your past, you would not be who you are now. You have become what you are *because* of your past. Be proud of who you are now. I mean it! You could even wear a special ring that signifies the bond with YOU. Imagine you are "married" to you. You already said "I do" when you were on the Other Side and decided to come into this life. Now renew your vows. With deep love and gratitude. Loving and respecting yourself means loving all other beings as much as you love yourself whilst refusing to allow yourself to be treated badly by anyone. It is the exact opposite of an egotistic, selfish or aggressive attitude towards the world.

❖ Write a love poem or a Valentine's card for yourself. Write a poem about how wonderful and unique you are. Display it next to your bed or put it under your pillow.

❖ Write a DEAR JOHN letter, expressing your anger and hurt freely. Burn it, keep it, but don't send it. This should be a cathartic exercise just for you.

❖ Write a fairy tale about your heartache. Make yourself the princess, or the prince and, using symbols, express your story in a magical way. Let it end with you finding true love. This is the ending you ultimately desire for yourself, isn't it?

❖ Be patient. Ask your angels for help. Take time out to experience solitude and to clear your mind and heart. You will know when you are ready for the next adventure. Don't push fate, be patient. Know that God and the angels are working for you behind the scenes.

> Heartache is a part of life.
>
> Grow from heartache. Develop a close relationship with yourself. Recognize your beauty and uniqueness and remember they were not good enough for you!
>
> Be patient and ask the angels to help you find your ideal partner.

I once asked my spirit helpers if my romantic ideas about love were stupid and unreal. This is what they said:

What you call "romantic" is the expression of pure love as we find it here in Heaven. We are bathing in this love all the time, we are It. Your recollection of these ideas, feelings and experiences is what makes you a Soul and not a body. Love is you, whether you are in spirit or manifest form. The more we remember it, the greater our chances of ever achieving and living it in life. So, no, your ideas are not stupid or unreal, they are the only thing that is real.

About being single

❖ If you are single, rejoice! Use the time to get to know yourself. Who are you? What are your unique talents? Your dreams? Your likes and dislikes? What is the deepest desire of your heart? What kind of a relationship do you want, if you want one? How do you want to feel in that relationship? Explore all the things you can do on your own, learn to like your own company. Go to the theatre, a museum, or the cinema on your own, go shopping, for a walk, join a gym, do charity work, learn to dance. Do whatever makes you happy. This way, you will never be dependent on another person, you will always know that you can be happy on your own. Being alone for me does not equal being lonely, rather it equals infinite freedom.

❖ I believe that it is important to know yourself and love and accept the person you are before you even start thinking about relationships. The more you love yourself, the more love you experience and the more love you can share with the world/others/ your (prospective) partner.

❖ Just because you do not have a partner in your life does not mean that there is no love in your life. Put love into everything you do. Love is in your work, your hobbies, your family, your friendships, your pets, your cooking and most importantly – you!

❖ I believe that it is better to have no partner than to be with the wrong one. I'd rather spend time alone, enjoying my own company and experiencing complete freedom than being manipulated and hurt in a relationship.
I have yet to meet the man of my dreams, but I have enough faith in God and in life to know that our paths will cross at the right moment in the right place. In the meantime, I am enjoying spending

time by myself, with myself, doing the things I enjoy doing, reflecting on my life and working on my spiritual side uninterrupted. Thus, I fill the solitude with meaning.

❖ You are unique – why expect to find someone like you?

We are all unique. We have unique memories, emotions, talents, feelings, ways of dealing with things, likes and dislikes. No-one in the whole world is like you. Furthermore, though opposites may attract at first, complete opposites cannot be happy with each other over a long period of time, unless each partner is ready to compromise (a lot). I therefore suggest wishing for a partner who shares your dreams and visions, your morals, your outlook on life, as well as many of your likes and dislikes. Many elements *must* and will be different, as people are all special in their own way. That brings with it some variety and excitement.

Whether you are single or in a relationship, remember to stay true to who you are and respect yourself.

Love (your partner like you love) yourself.

Remember you are unique. So is your partner.

❖ Work relationships

"Nearly all men can stand adversity, but if you want to test a man's character, give him power."
(Abraham Lincoln)

* * *

I have respect for authority. That's why I have always found it difficult to have a friendship with my superiors, or, in fact anyone I work with.

Work relationships are almost always connected to the aspect of power – who has power over whom and how are they using that power? Are they using it fairly, wisely, morally or are they suppressing other people's input and viewpoints by being authoritative, selfish, dominant or controlling?

Due to financial responsibilities, it is not always possible to resign and leave an unhealthy work situation. Most of us have bills to pay and/or mouths to feed, so we need to find ways of dealing with power struggles and difficulties.

I know from my personal experience that it takes enormous courage, strength and determination to transform a complex power struggle, and it is a good idea to ask the angels to assist you. You may be surprised at the miraculous changes in you and the other person.

When I started working as a teacher in England, I had a Head of Department who was my age, pretty, successful and a good teacher herself. However, she had control issues. She would micro-manage the department in such a way that I was most unhappy to say the least. I had no creative freedom in my job plus every bit of joy was stifled by her. I knew that my boss was unhappy inside due to personal circumstances. Her inner state of discontent, desperation and emotional stress was reflected in her daily conduct with students, as well as some members of staff, me included.

Whilst being compassionate I refused to be treated unfairly by her. So one day I decided that I had had enough and, having spoken to my union, told her about my rights as a teacher, and where her rights as a Head of Department ended. After that she cried, and from that moment on, she started respecting me. I had stood up for myself and shown not my teeth and claws but my true self which was very strong and powerful! And I had done it not to be mean, it was self-defense!

Some time later when she became pregnant and knew she was going to go on maternity leave, we developed a positive bond with each other. I was working side by side with her, moving the department forward – she had even made me Second in Department! We thanked each other constantly for each other's input in discussions and for each other's support. When she went on maternity leave I gave her thoughtful presents and organised a party for her. Thinking back to where we started from, that is remarkable. My feelings towards her had changed. I felt no resentment towards her whatsoever. I had turned the situation around by showing the world my true strength by standing up for myself, and she had started valuing my strength as a person and the fact that we shared many ideas, talents, and passions related to teaching. We parted in peace, valuing and respecting each other.

If that is possible for me, it is possible for you, too. Here are my tips on how to turn things around in a power struggle.

Give all your worries to Heaven – worries about losing your job/money/reputation; accept that whatever you do or say, you can never make a fool of yourself; ask the angels for help; pray, meditate, be creative/artistic in your personal life to remind yourself of the fact that your true strength lies underneath all the rubbish you deal with on a daily basis; love and value yourself for who you are. This will help you gain strength and confidence: Start with telling yourself little things like "I like my hair" and then move forward from there.

Try not to judge your opponent – you have both chosen to learn and teach (even if they don't want to learn – it's a matter of free will, if they refuse to learn, it's their problem!) each other something, and that lesson can best be taught and learnt if you don't judge but accept and acknowledge whatever they're doing or saying; recognise that the core of their soul is pure and light like yours (even "dark entities"[4] go back into the light when they are ready) and their lessons are unique like yours.

Recognise that the situation may be rooted in a past life and it reappears in this life so it can be transformed once and for all; appreciate all the things that are going well in your life at any particular moment – even if it's only things like "I have hot water at home" or "I can read" – remember there are many people who would rather be in your shoes right now, even with all the rubbish and chaos that's going on! Meditate on the soul connections you share; visualize your life the way you want it (excluding the conflict, and even excluding the person). Focus on what the true desire of your heart really is. Don't get distracted with the rubbish.

With all that, remember that even if you are ready to learn the lesson, the other person might not be. If that is the case, recognise your own pure intentions, and allow your opponent to learn the lesson another time from another soul. It is not your task to force any learning on them if they are not ready to accept it. In this case, avoid them when you can, and focus your thoughts only on YOU and what brings you happiness.

---

4   Sylvia Browne *Phenomenon*, pp. 87+

> Dealing with a power struggle at work can be a trying experience, teaching us about faith and patience.
>
> Try to keep your options open (Is there another job out there?) whilst standing up for yourself. Don't allow yourself be victimised.
>
> Pray for the situation to dissolve in a positive manner for all involved.

❖ The relationship you have with yourself

"When you cannot get a compliment any other way pay yourself one." (Mark Twain)

"We'll do it all. Everything. On our own."
(Snow Patrol, Chasing Cars)

"What lies ahead of us and what lies behind us are tiny matters compared to what lies within us."
(Ralph Waldo Emerson)

* * *

The most important relationship in your life is the one you have with yourself. Here on Earth, it may not always be easy to love yourself, as you may be self-critical, putting yourself down for the way you look/think/feel/speak/... - the list can be endless. Remember that you have chosen your body, your colour of hair and eyes and skin, your height, your weight, everything before you incarnated.

Therefore, learn to love yourself, to like yourself! Start liking your own company, spend time with yourself, get to know yourself, pamper yourself, speak nicely to yourself. It is like being in love with yourself, loving yourself so deeply that you don't want anyone to hurt you and you won't let yourself hurt you, either.

Above all, you are stuck with you, no matter what, for eternity. So you must work on developing a loving and kind attitude towards yourself. Loving yourself, liking the person you are in this life, is the only chance you have for real happiness. If you are hard on yourself you are not helping anyone. Try to forgive yourself for mistakes you may have made, your angels and God have forgiven you already. Try to refrain from punishing yourself with unkind words or actions.

Self-love, however, is not to be confused with an arrogant and selfish personality or a self-image that puts oneself above all others.

❖ **Acknowledge the deep sensitivity you feel towards yourself.**

Accept the fact that nobody can understand you 100%, nobody knows you 100%. You are the only person ever to have lived your life the way you lived it, to have felt the emotions you felt the way you felt them and to have fought your way through difficult times in the way you fought. Nobody knows you like you do! Trust yourself, your inner voice, love and cherish yourself for who you are. You are unique, and you are learning your very unique lessons. Extremely sensitive and loving people might understand you to a certain extent, but at the end of the day nobody really knows you like you do.

When I received an invitation to a school reunion after 15 years, I was deeply shocked. For once, I could not believe how quickly 15 years had gone. It felt like it was only yesterday that I had left school and I had seen my teachers and fellow students for the last time. I have to say I was not too fond of my classmates, with a few exceptions. So I was quite happy when I left school, and I knew that I would never have to see them again. 15 years later, I could feel a lump in my throat just thinking about them and about what I had been like then. In those times, I was not really happy, I was not spiritual in any sense, I believe I was quite stern and serious about life and had zero confidence in my true me, even though I may have appeared confident in my learning and knowing. Maybe that was just a way of protecting myself from feeling hurt. I realised when I received the invitation that I still had some forgiving to do – forgiving myself for not seeing things the way I see them now, forgiving the others for making me feel bad about myself at times, forgiving myself for still not having accomplished what I really always wanted – a loving husband and a family. On the other hand I needed to congratulate myself for finding the true me and connecting with the core of my Soul, developing spiritually more than I ever thought and accomplishing many of my goals. I reminded myself that I had come very far, and that I would get where I needed to be next in life with joy, self-confidence and faith. I also felt deep gratitude towards all my teachers, friends and fellow students who had supported me on my journey, from the very beginning, believing in me and discovering and nurturing my talents.

❖ **Say no when people put demands on you that you cannot or do not want to fulfill.** Your own sanity must come before anything and anyone else, and you must be true to yourself. If you need peace and quiet to recharge your batteries or you need alone-time, say NO.

❖ **Do not compare yourself with other people, or indeed the challenges they face in their lives.** Though other people's life situations might seem trivial to what you are going through, for one thing you can't look inside them and see how they are really feeling. Also I believe that overall the degree of difficulty/hardship is the same for every soul throughout their incarnations. Remember at the end of the day what really counts is what we've learnt about love and all feelings related to it like forgiveness, kindness, mercy etc. Every path is unique.

❖ **Mark Twain once said, "We should live in a way that when we die, even the undertaker will be sorry."**

I agree with that. We must respect and value other people, and that starts with respecting and valuing yourself first. By *respecting* I mean being clear about your aspirations, your likes/dislikes, your true nature and standing up for your individuality. Don't justify your life to other people, it's your responsibility and your birthright to live it the way you want it. You were born with unique talents and wishes, and you must stay true to them. Otherwise you may experience depression or anger. The path to freedom starts within you, your heart, the place within you where you feel the most grounded, loving and powerful. That's where you need to draw your strength from. Not from other people. And I do believe that people will admire and respect you for it.

At the same time have a loving relationship with people around you, as well as with yourself. Give compliments, blessings, a smile, small tokens of appreciation etc. Give something to everyone you meet, even if it's only in your mind, and you'll get something back. And when you die, even the undertaker will be sorry.

❖ **At least once a day talk to your angels**, and if it's only something like "Good morning, angels". Also talk to your spirit guide – if you know his/ her name, add it, too! –, deceased loved ones, and your totem animal. It will help you connect more and more to the spiritual realm and it will lift your mood enormously and make you feel lighter, more loving and more powerful. Consequently, your faith in yourself, life and all the love that surrounds you will grow, and, as you feel stronger and become more loving, you will attract loving energies into your life to share your joy and happiness.

Some people recommend meditation at least once a day, which is also a good way of switching off and relaxing completely. Personally, I do believe that if you have a very busy life, even acknowledging the spirit world will be enough, and if you start to feel the need for more time and peace, you can always actively make time for meditation. Go with what you feel – meditation should never be a task or seem forced! If it feels onerous, stop immediately, and do something else.

❖ **A depression is nothing but a STOP sign life throws at us**.
We are then forced to rethink our lives, to make clear decisions on how we want life to be, on what we want and what makes us happy. Once we are clear about that, we can start working towards our goals with a strong belief that life is there to help us, our angels and visible and invisible friends will make transformations possible for us, and we can live life in a happy way. A depression also forces us to redefine ourselves, maybe our appearances,

our personality, our ideals, dreams, and passions. We come to a point where we realise that we have to make a choice: Do we want our dream or do we want the reasons why we can't?

❖ **Once you make a decision to move forward, to trust life** and to let go of anything that is holding you back, be it an emotional or a mental obstacle, you are ready to shine your light in the world. Ask for guidance constantly and bless and thank whenever you can. You are now on the "EAC" (East Australian Current) - like in *Finding Nemo*. You are being carried, and it's very intense and extremely exciting at the same time. You don't know where you're going except that where you are going is where your soul's true desire lies. You have faith and trust that the current is taking you there, and you don't really need to do anything. Just be. Enjoy the ride.

❖ **Do not sell yourself short**. Know your worth. Admit your strengths to yourself, and challenge yourself to work on your weaknesses.

❖ **Enjoy every moment and be thankful for what is already here.** Enjoy the little things, whenever you can, be grateful for all. Think of Kevin in *Home Alone2- Lost in New York* when he is lying on the bed at the Plaza, eating ice-cream and watching a film. He is completely at ease, in the moment, as he exclaims "*This* is a vacation!" We love Kevin in this scene because we wish we

Marii K. K. Zierhut

could be more like him, free of worries and fears –
and guess what, we can be. Now. Here. We CAN be
happy now. We must be happy now. This moment
is as good a moment as any.

There is nothing wrong with feeling happy and
content at this very minute.

Why should I love myself? What's in it for me? What does it actually mean?

Having a positive, loving attitude towards
yourself will make you feel better full stop.
You will stop feeling not good enough, guilty,
invisible, powerless. You will start taking charge
of your life, creating your life around you. And
what other world could you create around you
rather than a loving one? Think of the ripple
effect – just imagine how many lives you touch
with your light and how that light transforms
not only you but also them and ultimately the
world.

Life will always have its challenges. People
have to go shopping and wait in the checkout
queue, people will have to move house, even
jobs, people have clashing personalities, people
get ill, people die. Ultimately, what it all comes
down to is this: Wish for the skills you need
to help you cope with it all in a balanced and
loving way.

❖ **Write a list of things you enjoy, and each day do one of those things**:

Some examples from my list are:

- *Listen to music*
- *Have a bath*
- *Sit in the garden or on the sofa*
- *Watch TV*
- *Read a poem*
- *Go for a little walk*
- *Sing a song*
- *Play Candy Crush*
- *Change my profile picture on facebook*

As you make it a habit to spend a little quality time with yourself every day, you will feel happier and more confident about yourself.

The relationship you have with yourself is the most important one in all of your lifetimes.

Be gentle and kind to yourself, do things you enjoy and develop inner strength, faith, and love for the person you have become.

Connect with the Core of your Soul by working on your spiritual side.

❖ **About gratitude**

"We can only be said to be alive in those moments when our hearts are conscious of our treasures."
(Thornton Wilder)

"Gratitude is not only the greatest of virtues, but the parent of all others." (Cicero)

* * *

Tell yourself, "I love you; for better, for worse, in sickness and in health. I deserve happiness in my life. I have the strength to transform or walk away from any negativity. I have angels by my side who guide me. I am grateful."

Why is gratitude important?

- By acknowledging the here and now you are also acknowledging your own existence in this world at this very moment. It's like saying "I am grateful, therefore I am." In other words, you realise that you exist and you claim your place in this world.

- Another reason – especially important when dealing with other people – is that gratitude opens hearts and expands our loving energy.

- Gratitude brings people closer together.

- Gratitude lets you feel the joy of the present moment.

You might want to start a "gratitude journal", a book where you write every day what you are grateful for. You could even include things in the future you are grateful for now, things you hope to attract. This might work for you.

I once kept a gratitude journal for a year. This did not work for me, it did not help me personally, but it may help you.

2009 was a particularly tough year for me, and writing down things I was grateful for felt a bit like a joke, even though I always KNOW that I am grateful for so many things! I believe it is better to know and say it in your mind every now and then than to force yourself to write it down, especially if you are going through a difficult time and trouble and disappointment are all around you. Instead work on spending quality time with yourself and loved ones.

Do something you enjoy every day for yourself and by yourself.

Develop an attitude of gratitude but do not force yourself, especially if you are going through a rough patch.

❖ About reflection

The idea of starting a "journey book" I absolutely love!

I would encourage you to dedicate a diary to your journey. Fill it with thoughts, dreams, pictures, photos, ideas, poems, drawings, prayers that come straight from your heart.

You cannot run away from yourself, so I might as well like yourself for who you are and enjoy spending time with yourself.

Any fallback just shows you a way not to do something. It has nothing to do with you not deserving happiness or you not being good enough.

You are good enough now.

Your happiness does not depend on your surroundings or on other people, it depends on how you treat yourself.

Be kind to yourself, be in love with yourself infinitely.

Keep a diary about your journey.

❖ Take out a hobby and be artistic

It is important to have interests and hobbies. That way you surround yourself with activities you enjoy doing and with people who share those interests with you. Plus it gives you something to do, it is an opportunity to learn new skills or discover long-hidden talents. Think of something you might like to do and then find out about courses in your area.

You could also volunteer and give some time a week to a charity of your choice.

Another good way to switch off from daily stress and work is to start being artistic! Nurture your creativity by making jewellery, painting, drawing, doing pottery, sewing, dancing, singing ...

There are so many ways of expressing yourself through art!

When you immerse yourself in something you love, you discover parts of yourself that would otherwise stay hidden. Painting to me is like meditation, I switch off completely. It is just me the brush, the canvas and colours!

Whether you decide to share your artwork with others or not, will be left to you. The important thing is that you do it!

Express yourself through art.

Go to a library or a book shop and let yourself be inspired by the variety of creative possibilities.

---

chapter 4

—— ❦ ——

About Children

"A baby is God's opinion that the world should go on."
(Carl Sandburg)

* * *

Children are the most vulnerable members of society, yet its only hope for a better future.

In my work as a teacher I have seen many children who come from loving homes where parents (regardless of whether they are divorced, separated, married or together) care for them and take responsibility for their education and upbringing. Such children are, generally speaking, a pleasure to teach and their academic progress tends to be steady.

I have also taught many children who come from dysfunctional homes where parents do not spend time with them, teach them right or wrong, or even provide a safe home. Children like that are often unable to behave appropriately in normal social situations, i.e.

the classroom. They need to learn to communicate properly, to develop respect and basic manners. Equally they need to learn to control their aggression and anger. They need guidance above all, and someone who encourages a positive self-image. When exposed to normal classroom situations, they often disrupt the learning of the others and may challenge or insult the teacher on a regular basis. In my opinion, dysfunctional children should be taught a limited amount of subjects in school and at the same time receive many hours of therapy with or without their parents.

Violent computer games and horror movies have a detrimental effect on young minds. Without even noticing it, negativity and anger accumulates in their psyche. Thus, they may become insensitive and aggressive adults.

Children need to re-learn to explore and acknowledge the wonder of being alive, loving, helping and supporting other individuals with an open heart. Instead of sitting in front of the TV or the Xbox, they need to spend time playing outside with friends, face painting, hand painting, playing sports, cooking, sewing, and developing interests and hobbies other than laziness and complacency.
Already illnesses like obesity and diabetes in children are rising, so why not change the way they spend their free time?

Sadly, as a teacher I have seen many families where parents are unable or unwilling to take responsibility for their own children, or even spend quality time with them. I always wondered who was going to teach such children about morals, love, sharing, etc if not them? Being a teacher, I always try my best to fill that void but I am not always successful.

I encourage you to express gratitude for your child's teachers. They have your child's best interest at heart, helping them to succeed to the best of their ability.

Parents' main aims should be to uplift and inspire their children from within, so that they recognise how wonderfully unique their personalities and talents are and that they can achieve any dream they have.

Children should learn to recognise and honour their natural capacity for wisdom, wonder, compassion and creativity.

❖ Indigo, Rainbow and Crystal children – Children of today

"What is a child of today?"

There are many books and definitions available of "Indigo, Rainbow and Crystal Children". However, I refuse to categorise children full stop! For me ALL children are equally special!

Children of today are, generally speaking, extremely sensitive, determined and bestowed with a strong sense of justice. For me they have clear values and ideas of life, which they are ready to outline to anyone who should think them special enough to ask about them. Many feel that they don't fit in, that they are different because of their emotional make-up. Many adults do not take the time to listen to them, or even to take them seriously, which is a real shame, as they need just as much guidance and loving encouragement as my generation and previous ones did.

Sadly enough, ever so popular horror films and war games mess with their young minds and often lead them away from recognising their true unique talents as well as their loving nature. In addition, many children have to wade through the waters of negativity, disbelief and insecurity prepared for them by their parents. This, however, is part of their chosen learning here.

Remember that anyone who crosses a child's path can make their lives easier by giving them loving guidance.

The one thing I feel that distinguishes children of today from older generations is that they have come to earth with a strong readiness to grow spiritually, and to grow faster than previous generations and to work for their own good and the good of others through bringing in innovative ideas as well as a lot of love and sensitivity.

Are all children like that, really? You may ask. In my opinion 99.9% are. Only once in more than 20 years of working with young people have I come across a truly malicious and harmful individual.

Nearly all children show the potential to be good, loving, caring and forgiving. Thus, they represent hope for a better future on Earth.

Growing up in this day and age *is* different from the energy of the 1970's when I grew up. Then no-one talked about angels, near death experiences, or the spirit world in general, even complementary therapies were only in their beginnings. Technology was limited compared to today. All in all, the vibrational energy we find on the planet today is undoubtedly higher than it was forty years ago.

Children deserve our respect, for they have come to incarnate on this planet which is so full of diversity.

Children deserve our loving guidance, time and dedication.

They are the future of the planet. We need to make sure as parents and educators that this future is a happy one for their sake and for ours.

chapter 5

About Work

"Choose a job you love, and you'll never work a single day in your life." (Confucius)

'Business!' cried the Ghost, wringing its hands again. 'Mankind was my business. The common welfare was my business; charity, mercy, forbearance, and benevolence, were, all, my business. The dealings of my trade were but a drop of water in the comprehensive ocean of my business!'
(Charles Dickens, A Christmas Carol)

* * *

Work is such an essential part of life. We spend more hours of the day working than we spend doing other things. Our thoughts may even be on work 24/7/52.
In the 1960s-TV series "Bewitched" where Samantha is a witch and can conjure up anything and work all sorts of magic, the only worry is that her husband might lose his job! How bizarre!

My advice would be to try to the best of your ability to choose an occupation you love, a job that incorporates and nurtures your talents. We all have different talents, and what makes one person happy, may not be the thing for you.

Do not only be money-oriented, listen to your gut feeling, follow the path of joy and make that your occupation in life. In addition, find an aspect of your job that offers you the opportunity to do good, give back, feel the contribution you are making to society.

This is, of course, an ideal scenario. In life we are faced with responsibilities that may create restrictions, and even a job you may enjoy doing in principal may bring with it colleagues and superiors you do not see eye to eye with.

Now this creates a dilemma. The question here is not how we got into such a situation. My advice would be not to analyse why you attracted this into your life!
I firmly believe that, while we may think we *choose* a certain place of work or an industry, there is a premeditated spiritual learning connected to it which we charted before we came into this life. It may be that something needs to be experienced again (similar to a previous lifetime), explored, transformed. This could be a relationship with a particular person or persons at the place of work or an experience connected to the work itself. In any case, experiencing restrictions and adversity in the workplace gives you an opportunity to grow, to evolve, to learn, to gain depth.

This does not mean, however, that we have to spend our lifetime continuing with this experience. We can learn and then move on. We are allowed to step off the stage at the right moment and seek something better.

How do we get out of a difficult work situation?

If experiencing adversity at work is part of your learning, I believe that "running away" will not result in happiness. Instead pause and think about your talents, your possibilities, your values and then look for a way to change the situation. This may not happen instantaneously. It may take time. But be open to change, keep your eyes open for opportunities, talk to others, surf the Internet for jobs, and, above all, keep your head held high. Try your best to stay positive!

There is one simple technique that is going to help you along the way – guaranteed!!! Whether you believe in God or the right time or destiny or not, do this and you will become a much happier person. Depression, hopelessness and powerlessness will vanish because your focus will shift to the positive, which will give you strength and a feeling of power.

Step 1 – Write down 5 things you like about your current job

I am serious! Firstly, you get paid to do the job, don't you? You get money in your pocket every month/week for doing your job. That has got to be positive!

How many weeks of vacation do you get a year? You get some paid time off, surely, that must be another advantage!

Maybe the working hours suit you? Maybe you meet people on a daily basis, some of or maybe all of them are interesting?

Maybe you can help people?

Maybe the lunch is good?

Maybe you are good at what you do and get enjoyment out of the job despite its drawbacks?

Find any five and write them down on a piece of paper.

Step 2 – Repeat to yourself in the mirror "I like my job because ..."

It is important to say it out aloud in front of a mirror, as it is a bit like saying it to someone else; it is a confirmation and a grounding exercise. It also helps you to accept the situation as it is.
Do this five times, adding the reasons in Step 1.

Say, "I like my job because ..."

Why does this help you? Because it grounds you, it helps you to accept a situation for what it is, and then shifts your focus to the positive. When we focus on the good, we feel happier and the situation becomes more positive. We gain strength and power and move away from feeling victimised.

Reflect on your talents and dreams

At the same time as acknowledging your present situation think of your gifts, your dreams. Write down all the things you want to contribute to society, all the things you want in your life and in your job. If you could start again, and if money weren't an object, what would you want to do?

Ask the angels to guide you towards opportunities that help you achieve this.

Above all, add a prayer to your Guardian Angel or spirit guide or spirit helpers in general and ask them to help you improve your work situation, so you can find the joy in life again. God hears every prayer, and no situation is ever hopeless. Acknowledge the help that is out there for you, though you may not *see* it, it is still there, and know that wheels are set in motion for you, there is a greater purpose to your life, this situation is only transitory. Ask for a sign, something that proves to you that there are hidden forces at work for you. Never stop praying for a miracle.

As mentioned in the chapter "About Work Relationships", I found myself in a work dilemma once when I had a boss who made my life very difficult. Needless to say, I felt very unhappy. I even asked the union to step in at one point, as I knew that some of the things she was demanding that I do were completely irrelevant to the job and caused me unnecessary workload and stress. I tried to find a job elsewhere and went to a number of interviews. Doing that, I realised that the workplace itself was actually good, she was clearly the only problem. I stayed away from her as much as I could, continuing to do a good job and leaving nothing on my desk any more for her to see. I prayed that my situation would change, as I felt this was the only thing I could do. Handing in my notice wasn't an option, as I had rent and bills to pay.

So I waited. And waiting was hard!!! You could now say that I chose this trying experience on the Other Side before I came into this life or that I attracted it here. I prefer the first explanation.

Going through this desert period has taught me clearly what it is like to be dependent on a job, to be stuck, to be treated unfairly, to feel sick when going to work, but I pushed through. I know now that I can get through it. I know that there is strength in me that I never would have found if my life had been easy, and I also relate to people who are dealing with a similar problem at present. I understand their feelings, emotions and thoughts.

What I do know is that faith can help, patience certainly will, and on a day-to-day basis, shifting the focus away from the negative is key.

What happened to my unpleasant boss?

She became pregnant three years (!) into this situation – so you know how long I had to wait – and I became her successor. We parted on friendly terms, she wrote me a good reference and I - being her boss for a few months before she left - did NOT make her life miserable. I became a boss that trusts others, believes in other people's strengths, is not threatened by them, and leaves others freedom to explore and develop their creativity. I have tried my best to become her opposite, and I am very grateful for this learning experience.

Choose a profession that reflects your unique talents and interests and therefore is an extension of you.

Focus on the positive aspects of your job, especially on a bad day or when faced with a difficult work scenario.

If unhappy in your job, look for a better solution. Ask yourself, "Deep down in my heart, what do I *really* want to do?"

Have faith.

Develop strength, depth and integrity along the way.

Be proactive and open, gather strength and keep believing.

❖ About the courage to change your line of work

Is taking a leap of faith a good idea? Should I take a risk and leave my current work situation to start something new?

You are the one to make that decision about your life. Generally speaking, I would advise people not to leave a secure job before they have got something else. Life has no safety net, it's up to you whether you want to jump.

Above all, keep focusing on your goals, keep at it, don't lose hope, stay patient. Good things often take time.

Develop the courage it takes to move on. Courage derives from the French word for heart "coeur". Do not lose sight of your heart's desire, of that one thing that you do well and can share with the world with joy.

Choose your confidants carefully and keep "heartbrakers" at bay. Heartbrakers are people who pull the brakes on your heartstrings and who tell you it is impossible.

Stop listening to the voices in your head that tell you you can't. When the time is right – and you will know when the time is right – take the leap of faith. Ask the angels for help, develop faith, understanding, humility, patience and depth in the meantime. A good cake needs time to bake and time to be decorated before it can be eaten and enjoyed.

❖ About the right time for change

I firmly believe that there is a way out of a difficult workplace scenario. In many cases, people change their place of work, or even their line of work successfully. Ideally you will find your dream job right away and earn your living doing what you love.

When is it too late to change your line of work? The answer is NEVER!

Here are some examples of celebrities who found their success late in life, so it is never too late. I chose celebrities to demonstrate this point, but having a breakthrough late in life can happen to anybody in any line of work, anywhere in the world. You may find some of these cases interesting and inspiring:

Louise Hay, motivational author and founder of Hay House, published her first book at 58.

Angela Lansbury, although a successful actress before, earned international fame with "Murder She Wrote" at 59.

Hubert von Goisern, Austrian folk singer, learnt to yodel at the age of 38 and published his first album at 40.

Andrea Bocelli started singing opera at 34.

Harlan Sanders, Colonel Sanders of KFC, had his breakthrough at 66.

Alan Rickman landed his first movie role at 46.

Peter Roget, publisher of the first Thesaurus, earned fame at 73.

When the time is right, inspiration will come and your life can suddenly change around, no matter how old or young you may be. Change may be sudden.

My favourite one – Sylvester Stallone, a struggling actor at the time, had a sudden flash of inspiration when attending a boxing match at the age of 30. He then wrote the Screenplay to Rocky in just 4 days! The rest is history.

Success may take a while to achieve but when it comes, it may be sudden.

Sylvester Stallone wrote the screenplay for Rocky in just 4 days at the age of 30, following a pivotal moment of inspiration.

When the time is right, change will be triggered.

Never stop being proactive and believing!

---

chapter 6

———————————— ✺ ————————————

About Wealth

"Money is power." (Anonymous)

"Money is like manure, of very little use except it be spread." (Francis Bacon)

* * *

Money is an essential part of life. We need it to buy food, shelter and necessary comforts like warm water and electricity. We use it to buy Plasma TVs, computers, furniture etc. Sometimes it seems that money is everything in the Western World. We judge a person by how much money they make.

A rich person is considered a "good catch" just because of their wealth (regardless of inner values?). We look up to a celebrity who has luxury properties in different countries in the world and travels in a private jet. It is a lifestyle many people dream and strive to have. Never to have to go to work again, complete and utter freedom!

Clearly, having money does make life easier. When you have money you do not need to worry about paying the rent or the mortgage, buying food, buying clothes, getting medical treatment etc.

However, research on lottery winners shows that coming into a large sum of money can be a curse, if the person lacks the emotional stability to deal with their sudden wealth and all the obligations and changes it brings about.

Let us not forget that there are many countries where people are mainly concerned with survival. In those countries learning new skills, getting an education and medical treatment are considered much more valuable than cash and possessions in general.

I believe that money is power. Having money gives you the freedom to buy what you want and to live your dreams, it gives you confidence and a good social standing, but with that come certain spiritual challenges. If I have freedom, how do I use that freedom, if I have power, how do I use that power? Do I use it to suppress others, to show others how influential and powerful I am?

"I am powerful, I am in charge, so no-one can or will tell me NO, I'm the one who has the say! People all want a part of me, they will do what I want, they'd better look up to me. I can say whatever I want to say, I can do whatever I want to do because I have the right to do that. I worked hard for what I have. I deserve it!"

Yes, you, or your relatives, who you inherited your wealth from, may have worked hard but life also helped.

Don't forget to develop a sense of humility. Regardless of how hard a worker you are, life needs to be on your side, life gives you the skills you need and allows you to make the connections you need to become successful. You are not better than the next man, just because you are richer! You are his equal, he is yours. Always remember that.

Sadly, I have yet to meet a wealthy person who is truly generous and caring. It almost seems that once you reached a certain level of wealth, you forget (if you've ever known) what it's like to struggle with money, what it feels like not to know how to pay your bills.

All the rich people I have ever met lacked sensitivity. Why should I pay for this for you? It's your bill, your obligation. I have even heard a rich person, who is a trained Angel Therapist, say to me, "Maybe you'll meet someone who will pay for you to go on that training course you'd like to go on. It can happen. You'll have to learn to receive. Your problem is that you are unable to receive." She said this without realising that she was the very person who could help me at that particular time!

Not that I expect or want people to help me out with money! I know that I can look after myself 100%. However, shouldn't we all look out for each other in some way? Should I ever be really wealthy myself, I have learnt from my time of financial struggles, and I vow to do things differently.

Furthermore, I would advise never lending anyone money. This is humiliating to the person in need and proven to end any friendship rapidly.

If you are in a position to help someone who is in need of money, give them money, don't lend them money! It's better to give someone £50 than to lend them £200.

> Money does make life easier, but it is no substitute for happiness.
>
> Try to keep control over your finances.
>
> The quickest way to lose a friend is by lending them money.
>
> Give generously, but do not allow yourself to be used.

❖ About charities

Whilst I am 100% in favour of charities, I believe that if you have people close to you who need money, this can be your charity. Don't go looking for the perfect charity to make your Christmas donation to, if you have a friend who was recently made redundant. Help them out instead or take them out for a nice meal and buy them something you know they don't have the money to afford themselves.

One reason why many wealthy people find it hard to share their wealth is that their possessions are their safety blanket, and they are scared to lose it all.

"If I give £100, I will lose £100, and they may expect me to pay for more and more for them in the future, just because I have more money than them. I don't want to keep paying for them! They are not my responsibility."

Wrong! Your fellow man is your responsibility up to a certain point, as long as they do not abuse your generosity. By giving, you are gaining, not losing. You gain other people's respect and gratitude and you become a role model.

What is wrong with paying for a friend once in a while or helping them out in a difficult financial situation, regardless of whether they ask you?

My aunt Reina is a wonderful example of just that. She was injured at her hairdresser's and got quite a large compensation from her insurance. Rather than putting all the money in the bank, she offered to help out the people close to her, who she knew were struggling financially, without them asking for anything. She gave me a substantial amount, just like that, to help me out, such a generous deed! I will never forget that!

Generosity is first and foremost. If you can't share what you have, you have nothing.

By sharing, you inspire others to want to share "back".

When I visited my brother in the USA in 2007, I was broke. I had just moved house and had no money to buy anything for myself, let alone invite him to dinner somewhere. I had a little bit of money which I was going to use to buy groceries. On arriving at my brother's apartment, he presented me with $200, stressing that he wanted me to use it to buy something nice for myself. I was so moved! I had tears in my eyes! I have to say accepting the present was not easy for me at the time, but I did. On that trip, my brother paid for everything! And I made a wish that one year later I would be able to pay him back – not literally, of course, but I wanted to invite him to lunch, dinner, pay for both our museum admission tickets and other things. And a year later, when I visited him in the USA again I did! It felt so good being able to treat him and I enjoyed every minute of it!

I once heard an inspirational story about a couple who won the lottery: They used the money to pay off their friends' mortgages as well as their own, and they still had the same friends and were very happy! What an amazing act of kindness and generosity!

Rather than giving money to a charity, help a friend or family member in need.

If you do pick a charity, choose one that you have a personal connection with.

❖ About giving, receiving and sharing

Ideally, you will achieve a balance between receiving and giving.

❖ *In 2004 my brother and I were both struggling financially. I had just started my teacher training in Surrey, and he was working near London. At weekends we used to meet in London and spend some time together. One time we couldn't resist going into one of our favourite stores at Piccadilly Circus – the huge HMV store! On walking in, we knew we would end up buying at least one CD each, possibly two or three, certainly more than we could afford.*

After spending some time wandering around HMV, we found ourselves in the queue at the checkout, each of us loaded with 4 or more CDs. Just as we were going to pay, I took one of my brother's CDs, wanting to pay for it and give it to him as a gift. My brother then immediately grabbed one of mine.

The point of the story is that we both paid the same amount we would have paid, had we just bought our own set of CDs but by exchanging CDs we actually got a gift and made a gift at the same time. Clever and sweet, isn't it?

❖ *My brother and I were taught to share everything from the very beginning, and we loved doing it. If we went to a shop and got a present from the shopkeeper – in those days quite common – say e.g. we got a sweet, we would always ask for another one for "my brother/sister" and make sure we had the same. We never rejoiced in having MORE than the other, we loved sharing everything.*

❖ *When each of us received a box of "Katzenzungen" chocolates (a box of little milk chocolate plates in the shape of what's supposed to be "cat's tongues", a common little present for children in those days) from family or our parents' friends, we always made sure we ate them one by one at the same time, so no-one would end up having more or less than the other at any particular time. We would always ask each other, "Are you eating another one now?" and then agree to eat one each.*

We did this naturally, automatically. And today we both know if one of us needs something whether this be money or other things, the other one is going to help them out and give them what they need (not lend, give). This will always be so.

Needless to say the responsibility to teach children about sharing lies with the parents. How can we achieve generosity in a society if it does not start in its smallest unit?

Above all, parents should make a point in treating all of their children equally.

I once overheard a student of mine say, "My sister was so mad last night because my parents gave me more pocket money for the German trip than she got when she went!"

Hearing this made me very sad. I know that my parents would never have done anything like that. They always treated me and my brother equally in every aspect. If ever one of us got more financial support than the other, it was because they needed it more, and my parents would always check if it was ok with the other one first.

Even if you are not wealthy at this point in your life, and you need to be vigilant about money, *imagine* you were rich! Pretend you have more than you need! How would you make a difference? Say to yourself, "One day *if and when* I am rich I will help ... I will do this ... "

The more abundance you experience, even if it may just be in your mind at the present moment, the more you will be able to give with an open heart.

Generosity is first and foremost. If you can't share what you have, you have nothing.

Give a present to a friend/ family member for no reason.

Pick your Christmas charity after you have thought about if you can support a friend/ family member in need first.

Giving and receiving should be balanced out, and if in doubt, give more.

Money is power and power can be abused easily if the ego is too big. Stay humble, no matter what.

Parents need to teach children about generosity and sharing, so that this world can become a place where people help each other without judging.

Don't feel bad about yourself because of your bank balance. Your bank balance is not YOU!

Imagine having lots of money. What would you do with it? How would you help others?

❖ About abundance

Let us now speak of abundance. Abundance is a feeling of absence of lack of any kind. It is often confused with wealth. Abundance means having plenty of all you need and being grateful for it. The feeling of abundance can be felt by anybody, regardless of their bank balance.

How often do you hear people say "count your blessings"? They are right. Abundance and gratitude are sisters, always together. Count all the things you have that money can't buy and you'll feel rich/abundant, happy and grateful.

Write down five things in your life money cannot buy:

Abundance is not the same as wealth, even wealthy people may not feel abundant. It's a state of mind where you know that you have plenty of what is dear to you.

chapter 7

About Dreams and Ambitions

"You have to have a dream so you can get up in the morning." (Billy Wilder)

"Be realistic, demand the impossible." (Che Guevara)

"Whatever you can do, or dream you can, begin it. Boldness has genius, power and magic in it." (Goethe)

"Wherever your heart is, there you will find your treasure. You've got to find the treasure, so that everything you have learned along the way can make sense." (Paulo Coelho, The Alchemist)

* * *

I believe that we have dreams in our hearts, so that we go out there and do the best we can to achieve them, praying and hoping for heavenly support along the way.

Our dreams are as unique as our personalities and Souls, charted before our life journey began with some pivotal moments and experiences along the way.

Speaking of dreams, I realise that I have got so tangled up in my earthly existence that I have almost forgotten to believe, to dream, to aim high, to soar. I am mainly a bundle of nerves, completely self-dependent without anyone to carry me and to make life easier for me. I have to fight each battle alone; I am the soldier and the marshal, the lieutenant and the king, all in one.

Yet, looking back at my life I do realise that there were a few very distinct times when I did experience a miracle, heavenly intervention or clear signs that directed me towards one of my dreams which has come true since. Yet, I am still hoping and praying for some other visions to come true, and as much as I can work for them, I know that ultimately my life is in God's hands. And the ifs and whens are God's call.

This is true for all of us.

Here is one example of divine intervention on my path:

Ever since I was a child I have known that I wanted to live somewhere other than Austria, where I grew up. I just did not know where. By the age of 17 I had visited many parts of Europe as well as the USA. At 18 I went to London, UK, for the first time. I fell in love with London and the UK on that trip. Now I know that my soul recognised a place it had known well in previous incarnations, but in those days I just knew that I wanted to live there. From then on everything I did was directed towards getting me there. At 25 I had almost finished my university degree, and starting to plan my career. It was then that my friend Mona told me about the ÖAD, an Austrian organisation dealing with the exchange of university lecturers abroad. I collected all the necessary information and put together an application. I did all this secretly, as I was not sure whether my parents and my brother would approve.

On the day I was planning to drop off the application (in those days you could not do this via the Internet; you had to post it or deliver it in person) I suddenly had doubts. How was I going to do this? Did I have the money? Did I stand a chance against all those other candidates? Wasn't I just making a fool of myself? I was wandering around the Kärntnerstraße area in Vienna, pondering what to do. Then, suddenly, in front of me an old man dropped his walking stick. I went over to pick it up for him, and he said to me in English (!) "Thank you."

I was speechless! In the middle of Vienna there was an old man speaking English to me!!!????!!!! This must be a sign! Following this incident, I immediately dropped off my application and ended up getting a job in the UK with the ÖAD, even though it was not the one I had originally applied for.

Believe in your dreams, ask your angels to guide you towards them. Stay hopeful no matter what. Do your bit, let God do the rest.

- Visualise living your dream.

- Ask for the angels to help and guide you.

- Go where the joy lies, not where the money lies – Prosperity will follow if you walk the path of your happiness.

- Take risks but be smart, stick to your values and beliefs and act according to your inner voice/ gut feeling.

- Have a sense of humour.

- Remember that your will can only take you up to a certain point. Have respect for your destiny. If success turns into failure, this is the lesson you've set out to learn. The true lesson is in learning from your actions and not to get caught in the same trap twice. Accept with humility whatever happens and grow from it. Failure always brings you closer to your core – success often lures a person away from their heart and confuses them. Ideally, failure will ground you, success will give you wings. Take the lesson for what it is and keep walking with pride and gratitude.

> Follow your dreams.
>
> Be open to signs and omens along the way.
>
> Remember the road to your dreams is the one you are walking.

chapter 8

About Suffering

"I do not believe that sheer suffering teaches. If suffering alone taught, all the world would be wise, since everyone suffers. To suffering must be added mourning, understanding, patience, love, openness and the willingness to remain vulnerable." (Mark Twain)

"Maybe God created the desert, so that man could appreciate the date trees." (Paulo Coelho, The Alchemist)

"No pressure, no diamonds." (Thomas Carlyle)

* * *

The angels told me about suffering:

Suffering brings you to you, it forces you to confront the limits of your consciousness. In suffering, there is only you, no-one else who feels what you feel like you feel it. It's personal and therefore leads you to the core of your own soul. It's the vehicle of transformation. But transformation need not occur. Some souls choose not to grow. Some choose to ignore, to cover up, to hurt others, so they feel less pain in the process.

At a different time, I had the following conversation with the angels:

Do you communicate with me through my intuition? Can I trust my inner voice at all? So many times my inner voice has failed me.

Your inner voice is a Divine Channel that is connected to your Soul's learning, like an umbilical cord. Sometimes you want to avoid painful lessons but you can't. They are pre-determined and carefully laid out. Your intuition knows what to do. You know what to do.

So I can't ever avoid pain and suffering?

Sure, you can. If that is your wish. You have learnt from the past, haven't you? Would you step into the same pile of dog poo twice? Would you seek out the next pile of dog poo, just to step into it? No, of course not! You'll make sure of it and we are at your service.

How can you make sure of it, if you say you can't intervene?

We can save you from disaster but we can't change your chart, your learning for this lifetime is a chance for you to accomplish that which you have set out to do. Your dance is of your own choosing, as are the dancers who dance with you. And the locations and the music. But of course we can help, just ask us! We can help and will, if you ask.

Pain and suffering never make any sense. Still, as we go through life, we may have to endure our body's reactions to outside influences and emotional breakdowns.

Painful experiences such as illnesses and emotional suffering I definitely could have done without! I have learnt, however, that I can come through extreme pain and suffering and that there CAN BE an end to it! I am strong enough to come out on the other side, and I sincerely thank all the Souls on Earth and in Heaven who were by my side in difficult times.

Try to protect yourself from detrimental influences from the outside. Ideally, take 5-10 minutes every day to cleanse your aura by meditating or simply by breathing in white or golden light and exhaling all the negativity of the day.

> See suffering as a chance to grow.
>
> Refuse to live a life of suffering, make a conscious decision to ask the angels for help, and do all in your power to make your life better and easier.
>
> Take 5-10 minutes every day to relax and do cleansing breathing exercises to release stress.

———— 🐚 ————

chapter 9

About Forgiveness

"In diesen heil'gen Hallen kennt man die Rache nicht.
Und ist ein Mensch gefallen, führt Liebe ihn zur Pflicht"
(In these hallowed halls revenge is unheard of. And
if a person has fallen, love will guide them to duty.)
(Wolfgang Amadeus Mozart, The Magic Flute)

"Nobody is perfect." (Billy Wilder, Some Like It Hot)

"Always forgive your enemies; nothing annoys them so
much." (Oscar Wilde)

"Not all treasure is silver and gold."
(Captain Jack Sparrow, Pirates of the Carribean)

"It is useless to meet revenge with revenge: it will heal
nothing." (J.R.R. Tolkien, The Lord of the Rings)

* * *

When someone deliberately hurts you, it shows you
a great deal about them. They reveal their insecurity,
their rudeness, their dishonesty, their cowardice, their

disrespect of others, their lack of social skills, in a nutshell (the dark side of) their true nature.

At our core, we are all good and pure and loving[5]. Sadly, however, many people have forgotten their loving core. Instead they feel comfortable nourishing their ego, and adhering to the rules of society, or, in fact, to no rules at all. Thus, they choose to cling to false values as if they were their security blanket.

In every act of hurt, there is a message for us, a possibility for us to grow.

When working as a teacher, my boss one day told me that the outfits I was wearing to work were inappropriate. My clothes were a pair of black trousers and a colourful top, so he was completely wrong to tell me I was inappropriately dressed, especially because other members of staff were dressed in a similar way. I could have gone down the route of starting a long discussion about other members of staff wearing this and that and why they are allowed to and I am not etc. but I decided not to do that.
To be judged by my appearance and unjustly criticised for it was totally incomprehensible and deeply hurtful to me!

---

5   In *Phenomenon* Sylvia Browne outlines her theory that there are "dark entities" whose intention it is to remorselessly destroy all light (goodness, love) around them. Such entities are worked on by loving spirits and will in the long run return to the Light. (Sylvia Browne *Phenomenon*, pp. 87+)

I went home and asked the angels for advice. They told me that any time someone is rude or disrespectful to you they are revealing a lot about themselves and they are so tangled up in their earthly existence that they are unable to acknowledge their divine nature any more, and when they see it in someone else, it frightens them and they react the only way they know how – by suppressing the light, i.e. by finding something they can hurt you with.

On the other hand, the angels told me that I should start wearing dresses and exploring other types of clothes, and that I was going to enjoy doing that. They told me that they would lead me to clothes that would complement my body and that I could afford.

And indeed they did – two months later, by chance, I stumbled across the perfect new wardrobe for me which matched my budget perfectly.

As much as you can, try to understand why someone hurt you, why they have so much insecurity or lack of love in their heart that they can forget that before God we are all equal.

Try to forgive them, for if you don't, you will be bound to that person/energy henceforth. Forgiveness sets you free, it helps you to let go and move on.

If you have to call that person a name in your mind when you speak or think about them, no problem. This can help you get rid of your negative emotions more quickly.

The important thing is to eventually forgive others here on Earth, for in Heaven we all love each other and there is no such thing as hard feelings between two souls. Therefore, the important time to make peace is in this life to make yourself free for your future. Don't let others hold you back; don't give them the satisfaction of pulling you down to their level!

It is also possible that others hurt you unwittingly, and that you (have) hurt others without realising it. We cannot help that. Nobody is perfect. Try to avoid it, though, by working on your sensitive and compassionate side.

Sometimes you hurt people unintentionally, and sometimes people hurt you unintentionally. That is a fact of life. Accept it, forgive them, forgive yourself, and move on. And remember there is always a reason behind every action.

Therefore, as bearing grudges is negative energy, it will take you down to a low level. It is also extremely unattractive to walk around with a grudge on your face or in your energy field.

At a training session for health products I was selling at the time an elderly lady came up to me and announced that she was "very disappointed that I never called her and let her know how I got on." Looking at her, I had no idea who she was or what she was talking about until maybe 30 seconds later, and I exclaimed, "Dancing! I know you from dancing! And yes, I remember Jane (our dance instructor) gave me the phone number of a relative of yours in Canada. Yes, I remember! But I don't think I rang him in the end ..." I had not seen that woman in two and a half years! The story slowly came back to me. She repeated one more time that she was disappointed in me and then stormed off. I could not believe her rudeness, nor her aggression. She was clearly not in a place of love. If she had been, she would have known that there are reasons behind people's actions and that I never willingly hurt her by not ringing her. She had in fact passed on someone's phone number to me at a time where I was desperate to get out of my job. Her cousin ran a translation company in Canada. I was feeling low at the time, and finally decided that no way was I going to Canada, and translation work was not going to make me happy. So I never made that phone call to her relative, and yes, I did have a reason why. And I never rang her either because I was terribly depressed at the time. Again there's your reason. Had she rung me and expressed a genuine interest in my situation, I would have been so thrilled and grateful, and a beautiful friendship might have developed. The possibilities of loving actions are endless ...

My advice therefore is: if you're mad at someone and you cannot talk to them about it for whatever reason, let it go – do not bear grudges, and especially not for two and a half years! And always look for the reasons behind people's actions. I promise you'll always find them.

Forgive yourself when you've made a mistake. Beating yourself up about it won't help anyone.

As far as abuse, war and general violence are concerned, I do not understand how people can inflict horrible crimes on others, let alone why a soul would chose to be on the receiving end of it. This is a question that keeps me awake many a night.

All I can do is to continue to have faith in God that nothing happens without a reason and to pray for both victims and offenders.

Forgiving others will set you free.

Develop your sensitive side, be compassionate.

Don't be hard on yourself. We all make mistakes from time to time.

Pray for victims and offenders. There are so many things we as humans can't fully understand. Violence is one of them.

---

chapter 10

--- 🐚 ---

About Spirit Helpers

"There are more things in heaven and earth, Horatio, than are dreamt of in your philosophy."
(William Shakespeare, Hamlet)

* * *

Every human has a "spiritual glam squad" with them all the time. They communicate with us through intuition, our conscience and in our dreams.

Have you ever pondered on what to do about a certain situation and suddenly you know exactly what to do, who to call, where to go? Have you ever avoided a certain path because you had a bad feeling in your stomach? Have you ever done something and afterwards felt that you may have done the wrong thing and hurt someone in the process? Did that entice you to put things right? Have you ever had an intense dream, packed with emotions, and when you woke up you felt like you'd learnt something? Maybe you even saw a deceased loved one or an angel in your dream who gave you a message?

All of the above would be communication with the spirit world.

Please refer to the guided meditation at the end of the book to connect with your personal spirit helpers.

So who makes up your spiritual glam squad?

❖ Your permanent spiritual glam squad

- **Your Guardian Angel**

  Your Guardian Angel is with you from the beginning of your earthly existence to the day you die, which is when you are united with the spirit world again. Angels come directly from God. They have no free will as such, their purpose is to give unconditional love and to help any way possible to alleviate our incarnational learning. Your Guardian Angel loves you unconditionally, no matter what, and his/her greatest joy is seeing you happy. Acknowledge your Guardian Angel and thank him/her for their guidance and love. If you feel you want to call him/her by his/her name, my advice would be not to seek out a psychic but to choose a name you love in your heart. Should that name not be their exact name, your Guardian Angel does not mind. Being with you is such a joy to him/her, your happiness is his/her only concern. No matter what choices you make in life, your guardian angel will love you. He/She will never desert you.

Is your Guardian Angel male or female? My view is that angels are both male and female at the same time, each angel being individually equipped with either more male or female properties and energies.

Angels never incarnate but they may assume a human body if it is necessary to help us, or even to save our life. Many people whose lives have been touched by a genuine angel report "looking back to thank the individual but they were suddenly gone."

According to Lorna Byrne[6] Guardian Angels are spectacularly beautiful and lightful, and every person has one. Sylvia Browne[7], on the other hand, believes that "dark entities", souls who have decided to turn away from God, committing horrible deeds without repentance, lack such a companion. This was verified by a psychic child I have worked with. I personally believe that to be true, but in the same way, such a soul would be surrounded by loving spirits who will try to get him "back" and make him

6   Lorna Byrne *Angels in my Hair*, p. 16

7   Sylvia Browne *Phenomenon*, pp. 87+

see the right path, however hopeless that task may be. In the end, "dark entities" will become light-ful again. Such is my belief.

- **Your Spirit Guide**

  Before we incarnate we pick a soul that will be our spirit guide in the lifetime to come. It can be a soul we are particularly connected with due to other lifetimes, our "twin flame" (a soul that was created at the same time as you and complements you completely), or even a soul we don't know yet. We discuss our chart with them, and when we die our spirit guide is amongst the first to greet us on the Other Side. Our spirit guide is there for us to guide us through this lifetime, and he/she never leaves us. In addition, we might have other temporary spirit guides, e.g. passed loved ones – permanently or temporarily. A spirit guide understands what we are going through in our incarnation, as they themselves, unlike angels, have walked the earth at least once. Your spirit guide has a name but won't mind if you give them a name you love to call them by. Your spirit guide is either male or female.

- **Your Angels**

  Angels are around us all the time, ready to protect and to help us with anything we need - all we have to do is ask. They want us to have peace and feel the joy and happiness life has to offer. They love us unconditionally and want us to be happy. We can ask for extra angels to be around us, or loved ones.

- **Archangels**

  The archangels are very powerful angels who can help us anytime, anywhere. They can protect and guide us and also help us to take action in our lives. We can call on archangels at any time, as they can simultaneously be with anyone who calls on them and can work alongside your guardian angels to assist you with whatever you need. Each archangel has a particular role but don't worry about calling on the "wrong" angel, there is no such thing.

Archangel	Healing
Michael	Fear, doubt, negativity, protection
Chamuel	Lost objects, anxiety, peace
Gabriel	Conception, pregnancy, childbirth, creativity
Haniel	Female cycles, clairvoyance, beauty
Jophiel	Beauty, organisation, art, fun
Metatron	Learning disorders, children, spirituality
Raphael	Illnesses, healers, addictions
Raziel	Spiritual and psychic blocks, past-life memories, manifestations
Sandalphon	Aggression, music, unborn babies
Uriel	Unforgiveness, new ideas, problem-solving
Zadkiel	Memory, mental functioning, compassion, forgiveness

Table from Doreen Virtue: *Crystal Therapy,* pp. 28+

- **Your Animal Spirit Guide**

  Before we incarnate, we choose our personal animal guardian angel – our totem animal. It is another guide who is there to help us through this incarnation, apart from angels and spirit guides. One's totem animal is an extension of some of one's personality or essence.

  Your totem animal watches over you. You may also wish to ask for the assistance of other animal spirits in addition, depending the challenges you are facing.

  Pets we have had in this lifetime or previous ones can also "jump in" and help us out.

  My animal spirit guide is a leopard. Ever since I saw "Bringing up Baby" as a small child, I have adored leopards. I am not keen on leopard skin fashion accessories, I just love the animal. To me leopards are the most beautiful and elegant creatures, representing strong energies of passion, beauty, fierceness, as well as gentleness.

❖ Additional - sometimes temporary - members of your spiritual glam squad

- **Unicorns**

  Unicorns are from the same heavenly realm as the archangels. They want to help us feel happier and make our dreams come true.

Their role is to inspire, give hope, empower and enlighten. Some unicorns have a golden horn, others a white one. Their energy is pure and gentle. Children particularly love and trust them. Many people feel a strong connection with ancient Atlantis these days. According to Diana Cooper[8] almost everyone on earth has had an incarnation in Atlantis. For a period of 1,500 years, the people of Atlantis maintained their purity and oneness with the Creator, and enjoyed amazing spiritual, psychic and technological powers.

Unicorns were the guardian angels of Atlantis. Every human would have their own unicorn with them to guide and protect them at all times. Therefore, you may feel a strong connection with Atlantis or unicorns. Unicorns symbolise pure, unconditional love, often referred to as "Christ energy". Ask to be guided and protected by a unicorn or unicorns, deepen that connection, if you feel this is something that resonates with your heart.

- **Ascended Masters**

  Ascended Masters are great teachers and healers, most of whom have had an incarnation on earth. They come from all cultures and religions. They specialise in particular qualities

---

8 Diana Cooper *The Wonder of Unicorns*, pp.48+; see also Diana Cooper *Discover Atlantis*

and they help bring out courage, love and transformation in everyone who is willing to listen and ready to live their life for the highest good of all. Call on them for guidance.

Some examples of ascended masters are Paramahansa Yogananda, El Morya, St. Francis of Assisi, Master Hilarion, Siddhartha Gautama Buddha, and Mother Mary.

When my friend Mona moved from Vienna to Sheffield in 2010 she had a job teaching German at university, but she still needed a place to live. As she was on a limited budget, she found it hard to find a property to rent that ticked all her boxes. Finally, she viewed a flat she liked and signed the contract late on a Friday evening, following her intuition and inner voice. Immediately afterwards she drove to Warwickshire to visit me, and the plan was that I was going to go to Sheffield with her the following week and help her move.

Over the weekend she started having doubts about the flat. Was it the right size? Was it clean enough? Was it really meant to be her home?

Looking for answers, she used my Doreen Virtue Ascended Masters Oracle cards set and picked a card. She picked St. Francis. The message that came with the card made no particular sense to her. It was about following her heart, but how should she follow her heart, if she was not even sure whether she had made the right decision when choosing the flat?

When we went to Sheffield the following week, we viewed the flat together. I thought it was light, friendly, and sufficiently spacious. Being nosy, I opened all the cabinets in the kitchen. Inside one of the cabinets there was a piece of paper stuck on which contained a poem starting with the words "Lord, make me an instrument of your peace, where there is hatred, let me sow love ..."

This is, of course, the beginning of the famous prayer by St. Francis of Assisi, who was with Mona to give her assurance that she had successfully found her new home!

- **Fairies**

  Fairies and other nature spirits remind us to look after and respect the Earth. They are able to help us to have more fun and not to take ourselves too seriously. They can also teach us to manifest our desires as well as help us take more care of the environment and its inhabitants, including the plants and animals. Fairies are bubbly, fun-loving, lightful, often even mischievous creatures who watch over nature. They love to sing and dance. There are many forms of nature spirits, but fairies and tree spirits I find the easiest to connect with. How to connect with fairies or tree spirits? Very simple, start talking to them, in your mind, tell them how beautiful they are, acknowledge their presence. Have you ever wondered why talking to plants makes them grow faster and develop more blossoms? If you have many daisies and buttercups and circles of mushrooms in your garden, this is a sign that fairies feel comfortable in your garden. You can't kill fairies when you mow the lawn, but just warn them beforehand, so they don't get frightened.

- **Loved ones who have crossed over**
  "When our bodies die, most of us experience the brilliantly lit tunnel, rising from our own bodies and leading more "across" than "up", at about a thirty-degree angle. We travel with gorgeous, weightless freedom through this almost sideways tunnel, never for one instant feeling as if we've died but instead feeling more thrillingly alive than we could imagine here on earth. All our anger, frustrations, resentment, and other negativity melt away, replaced by the peace and all-loving, unconditional understanding we remember and we are about to reunite with at Home."[9]

  Loved ones can return to us in spirit form to help and guide us, or simply to let us know they are alright.

  When they do, ask them to give you a clear sign that it is truly them!

---

9   Sylvia Browne *Visits from the afterlife, pp. 6+*

My good friend, spiritual teacher and physician Beate died a few years ago. She had played a major role in me developing my Hawaiian connection, and she had introduced me to past-life regression as well as guided hypnosis in general. She was a believer in my clairvoyant abilities and used my angel paintings in her work.

After her death I often wished that she would come back to me in a dream, so I could see her again and maybe even ask her some questions. One night after she had passed away I had a vivid dream of her. She appeared smiling lovingly from ear to ear, full of life, radiating such happiness and joy and goodness that I immediately knew that she must be fine on the Other Side. I asked her a question about my life, and she answered it. After that, I remember thinking in my dream, "If this is really you, give me a sign!"

When I woke up, I noticed that the pain in my right shoulder which had plagued me for weeks was suddenly completely gone! I could move my right arm without any pain – it was a miracle! I took this to be a sign from her, assuring me that it had really been her I "met" that night.

My dream encounter with Beate felt a bit like the end of the "Wizard of Oz" where Dorothy is back in her room. We see her ruby slippers beside her, and we know that though her journey was magic, it was not an illusion! The proof is in the slippers. The proof is in the sign that loved ones on the Other Side will give you.

❖ How to communicate with spirit helpers

You can consciously communicate with your spiritual glam squad through Oracle cards, meditation, or channeling. Channeling is the most open and the most unguided way. If you want to learn to channel, and you are scared to try it alone, look for a spiritual teacher you trust (See *About Psychics and Clairvoyance*). Open up more and more little by little, and when you are ready, you will start to receive the messages from your angels and other spirit guides.

It took me years of training with experienced psychics and spiritual teachers to build up my confidence before I had the courage to channel messages from the angels for the first time.

This need not be so! Many people may do this naturally, or they may learn this faster and/or at an earlier age already.

I personally only communicate with my angels and my spirit guide, and sometimes with nature spirits. I am uncomfortable starting a communication with deceased loved ones, even though they may at times tell me something anyway. I would not specifically call on them, though. I prefer going to the angels directly, who are close to God and will know my chart better than deceased loved ones, as the angels are on a higher vibration.

My spirit guide is such a humorous, loving wise man, I enjoy his words and guidance a lot. As he is a Native American shaman and spiritual leader I have known in at least one other lifetime, I have decided to call him "Manitou-a". He likes that name and may give me specific messages from time to time, starting the sentences with "Manitou-a says ..."

My advice to you would be to stick to what you feel comfortable with, and if you get insight into areas you are not comfortable with, ask the angels to help you see only the things that you can "handle".

At the end of this book you will find a guided meditation you can do alone or with a friend. Are you excited about receiving loving messages from the spirit world? One thing is for sure – your spirit helpers are excited to talk to you!

You are never alone. You are constantly surrounded by "invisible" spirit helpers, some of which come directly from God (like the angels, archangels and unicorns), and some of them have lived at least one life on Earth before (spirit guides, deceased loved ones, ascended masters).

Acknowledge their presence and ask them for guidance. Thank them for the signs you receive.

You put together your "spiritual glam squad" before incarnation, but some guides may come and go in addition to that, offering their help and love to you.

You can learn to communicate with them through Oracle cards, meditation or channeling. They subconsciously communicate with you in your dreams and through your intuition.

If you are a skeptic or a non-believer, your guides are there for you anyway, bringing you love and support when needed.

I once asked my spirit helpers who they were, and this is what they said to me:

We are your guides, the brothers and sisters you have chosen to be with you when you are here in this life. Some of us come and go, some are here all the time. Our job is not an easy one, we agreed to this before you came. You agreed to this plan before YOU came. We said we'd do it together, for you, with you because of you. As a Soul you are old and young at the same time. You always are. You exist forever and since forever. This moment is not all, this moment is just an experience in time and space – you have asked us for help and we have heard you.

❖ Orbs

Orbs are balls of light which may appear in modern-technology photographs. They usually have a clear ring of light on the outside and they are round, sometimes perfectly shaped and sometimes the shape looks slightly distorted or elongated. In my experience Orbs appear only when a flash is used. Orbs can move (in two consecutive photos they may be in different places or they may show a line of light) and shine in colours, e.g. green or blue are quite common.

Orbs are distinctly different from photos featuring the reflection of sunlight.

What are Orbs?

Orbs are spiritual energy on photo. Angels, spirit guides, deceased individuals, ghosts, unicorns or fairies are able to lower their frequency and show themselves on film in this form.

Frequently they show themselves in nature, around children and animals, in places of high energy where many people come together (e.g. family gatherings, celebrations, dance and music festivals) and at historical sites.

I believe that anyone using the right equipment is able to photograph an Orb, if those high-vibration energies are willing to show themselves at that particular moment. However, not everyone is able to recognise or even to see one.

Before I knew of Orbs, I took many pictures containing them, but it was only when I became aware of Orbs through reading about them in *Enlightenment through Orbs* by Diana Cooper that I looked back at my photographs and found many Orbs in them.

According to Diana Cooper, your Guardian Angel is usually an Orb close to you in a photo.

Orbs are spirit energy on photo.

chapter 11

─────────── ✺ ───────────

About Psychics and Clairvoyance

"Dreams are today's answers to tomorrow's questions."
(Edgar Cayce)

"Maybe the paths you each shall tread are already laid before your feet, though you do not see them."
(J.R.R. Tolkien, The Lord of the Rings)

"The world is changing: I feel it in the water, I feel it in the earth, and I smell it in the air."
(J.R.R. Tolkien, The Lord of the Rings)

* * *

Psychic people are fascinating. They see, feel and hear things that others do not, which gives them a certain degree of power over their clients.

Above all, no psychic, no matter how gifted they may be, is right all the time. They are only human, and they make mistakes, too. I love it when psychics acknowledge that they have made a wrong statement, and I respect them for it.

Beware of the following:

- Some clairvoyants will never admit that they have made a mistake and simply say something like "You had to hear what you heard at the time, so what I said was right and it was what you needed to hear." I think this is a cowardly and arrogant cop-out, and I would strongly advise you stay away from such people.

- Another thing I find alarming is when psychic people call themselves "healers" and claim to be able to cure any condition. That can never be! God gives his permission for a person to be healed or not, so no healer is able to use healing powers all the time.

- Beware of psychics who charge high fees. No-one should exploit a God-given gift for their own profit.

In my opinion, true psychics are humble. They are equipped with a sense of humour that stems from their deep connection with God and the spirit world in general, and they exhibit deep faith and respect for all life on Earth - humans, animals and nature.

No psychic will get predictions about their own life. They are living a human life, therefore they must err and learn like anyone else.

The aim for all of us should be to live life with infinite faith in God, which helps on one level but does not necessarily make life any easier.

Above all, rather than going to see psychics on a regular basis and putting your life and money into their hands, I suggest you work on developing your own psychic abilities. I believe that we all have a Sixth Sense and we can all connect with God, the angels, our spirit guides and other helpers in the spirit world, if we so wish. This process may take years to develop. It starts with a deep desire to look beyond. Before we can start the process, we first need to acknowledge that there is "more" out there.

Many people are afraid of "the invisible". This can be the case for many reasons. They may fear that the Other Side is dark, uncanny, or spooky. They may fear that crossed over loved ones will give them negative messages or haven't forgiven them for something they did or did not do while they were alive. They may even have past-life memories connected with tragic events following a psychic life or a religious one. I believe that most of us have lived at least one life in religious surroundings, which may or may not have been a happy one. Life in a convent, a monastery, especially in the Catholic Church, may have contained events of martyrdom, being burnt at the stake or tortured. Therefore, when spiritual subjects come up in this life, alarm bells go off in their minds and they know they want nothing to do with it, for it means pain and horror.

The more I started to open up to the "invisible", the more magical my life has become and the easier it is to go through "dark times". I know that there is hope out there and that I – like you - am loved unconditionally by my Guardian Angel, my spirit guide, other spirit helpers, my "spiritual glam squad", as I like to call them.

As a child I had psychic abilities. I remember sitting in St. Stephen's Cathedral in Vienna with my grandparents Dorothea and Ernst and KNOWING that it was going to be the last time that we would all sit there together. A few months afterwards my grandfather sadly died unexpectedly.

In my teens I was opposed to the idea that there was a God. I refused to believe in God, finding fascination in "Existentialism". In retrospect, that phase was me being an obstinate teenager, rebelling against my mother, who is clearly connected to the spiritual, being very religious and raising me and my brother in that way. My father to this day claims to be an atheist, even though he is a perfect example of a good and kind person with high values and morals.

Little by little, triggered by a painful dislocated coccyx, I opened up to the "invisible" - first to the more logical, energy-flowing forms like Chinese medicine, acupuncture and Reiki. After that came my first meditations, visualisations, and hypnoses. I also had a few visions. One time in my late twenties I saw a bright white light coming towards me at night when I was lying in bed. I was wondering to myself, "What is this light? It can't be the headlights of a car, as the window is on my right?" I winked and the light was gone. It was a beautiful moment.

It was not until my mid-thirties that I started to write messages down from the angels. By that time, I had connected to nature spirits by learning about tree and plant energies, as well as to angels, Ascended Masters, unicorns, and fairies.

I had never had the confidence before to channel myself, I had preferred to see psychics who did the channeling for me. However, they did not always do a good job.

Anyone can learn to communicate with the spirit world, and all of us are already doing this through our intuition, unaware of the fact that they we doing it. Have you ever had a psychic or prophetic dream? Have you ever just known something without being able to explain why and how?

One easy way to communicate with the spirit world is through Oracle cards. Nowadays, there are many Oracle card sets available. Pick a set you like and practise with it. It will help you open up to more complex ways of communication.

Not every communication needs to be as spectacular as writing down messages or seeing a vision.

Try communicating with the spirit world by doing the simple meditation journey at the back of the book.

Not all people who claim to have psychic powers have a good heart, so be careful who you trust.

Remember even the best psychics don't get it right all of the time.

Develop your own psychic abilities, so you can hear spiritual guidance yourself.

Follow the signs you receive and enjoy your connection with your "spiritual glam squad".

Open your heart to the love and goodness in you and around you.

chapter 12

———————— ✦ ————————

About Miracles

"I can believe anything, provided that it is quite incredible." (Oscar Wilde)

"There are only two ways to live your life. One is as though nothing is a miracle. The other is as though everything is a miracle." (Albert Einstein)

"Miracles do happen and they can happen to you." (Roma Downey, It's a Miracle TV show)

* * *

Winning the lottery, surviving a terrible accident, a turn for the better change of a negative situation?

What miracles have you experienced in your life?

I believe that we do not experience a miracle because we *attract* it; I believe a miracle occurs due to a combination of prayer, faith and pre-charted elements in our life.

Miracles remind us that sometimes all we can do is step back, let go and let God. Here are two miraculous situations I have experienced in my life:

In 2001 I moved to the UK, completely on my own. I had a job as a Foreign Language Assistant in Eastbourne on the South Coast. I booked a B&B for my first week, hoping I would quickly find a place to live. However, that was naïve thinking. My employer, who I had hoped was going to help me, did not show any signs of getting involved, nor did looking through the local newspaper prove useful. In those days, the Internet and mobile phones were only in the early stages, so all I could do was look in the newspaper and walk around and look for signs on houses. Every flat I viewed was either dirty, small, smelly or in an unfriendly area. In addition, prospective landlords would bombard me with questions about my earnings, job, and generally about my personal life. Every night I cried! I wanted to live in the UK, but why was it so difficult?

Then I remembered a story my Reiki teacher Helga had told me: Her daughter was looking for a room in Germany and had been unsuccessful. Then one day she went for a walk by a river and fell in love with a particular house. She noticed a sign that said "room available". Needless to say, she went in to enquire and she got the room.

I remembered that story as I was looking for a flat. On Friday of my first week I walked around Eastbourne in an area I thought was absolutely beautiful. There were many old Victorian and Edwardian properties, big mansions with huge gardens with trees and flowers galore. One house in particular caught my attention. It looked Victorian, with a paved walkway up to the front door, surrounded by an enormous garden with all sorts of trees, flowers, and bushes. It looked gorgeous! To live in such a house, I thought! As I took another step, I suddenly noticed a sign I had not seen before, as it had been obstructed by bushes. The sign said "Holiday apartments for rent" and a telephone number. I rang that number and left a message. That evening, I rang the number again. The lady I spoke to was so nice! She laughed and joked with me on the phone and we had a wonderful conversation. She did not ask me any personal questions, she was open and lovely and talked to me about the house. The house was an old Victorian house indeed and had been converted into eight flats. If I was interested, I could go to a viewing on the following day at midday and possibly rent a flat. Of course I was interested!

Needless to say, I went there the following day, loved the house and the people, and another day later moved into flat number 5, overlooking the garden. When I was at the viewing, I met some Germans who were my age who were in Eastbourne to study for a year. We became great friends and one of them is a good friend of mine to this day! Now that's a miraculous string of events, isn't it?

One Sunday evening in January 2003 I was driving on the M40 motorway on my way home to Stratford-upon-Avon after visiting my brother in London. Stupidly,

I was fiddling with the radio and lost control of the car, spinning a few times, and then finally crashing sideways into the central reservation barrier. As the car came to a halt, I realised that, luckily, no-one else was involved in the accident, nor was I injured (apart from whiplash). The car was totaled, and I am grateful to this day that nothing worse happened. I believe that this was a miracle and possibly one of my exit points (pre-planned moments of death)[10] that my Soul did not take.

I could go on writing about many more events in my life I would call miracles and I am truly grateful for. I am sure you have your own stories to share with people, too.

I am a firm believer in faith, and prayer and the fact that, no matter how hard the learning may be, eventually things turn around for us, all of us.

> The more you believe in miracles, the more you will notice miracles around you.
>
> Be grateful for the miracles in your life.

---

10 Sylvia Browne *Phenomenon*, pp. 115+

chapter 13

---- 🐚 ----

About Past Lives

"What we do in life echoes in eternity."
(Maximus Decimus Meridius in *Gladiator*)

* * *

We *are* not just a human body, we also have, or rather *are*, a Soul.

We often hear people say "She is an old soul." or "He has not got a soul." But what do we actually mean by that? Let us define the word "soul" in a spiritual sense first of all.

My "Aloha Coaching" student Will B., aged 12, defined perfectly what a soul is: "It's your spirit. It's who you are."

It is who we are and always have been and always will be, across all of our incarnations and on the Other Side, the very essence of our being which is spiritual and eternal.

❖ Past lives

Chances are you have been here before. It's not the first time that you have chosen to incarnate on Earth. Some souls are here for the first time, but most of us have lived here before. Many souls would never even go near this place, which is such a mixture of all things good and evil, the ultimate boot camp you might say. Instead, they choose to learn and evolve in other dimensions or on other planets.

To find out the first thing about your past lives, ask yourself this simple question: What are your likes and dislikes? Then expand on the following:

What are your fears and joys?

What kind of music do you like?

What kind of food do you like?

Which time in history do you feel drawn to or do you resent?

Which countries naturally interest you and which repel you for some inexplicable reason?

What are your main challenges in this lifetime?

Which people know how to push your buttons and why?

Which people do you love unconditionally?

The answers to these questions will give you clues about your past lives. In addition, you may meet people in your life you are drawn to immediately and there are some people you can't seem to warm towards. It is quite possible that that, too, may stem from a past existence.

Since incarnating on Earth, i.e. going into an existence in time and space, is particularly tough, we often incarnate together with groups of souls or at least one soul who we have known and loved before to help and support us, to be there for us, and to share experiences with, or even to complete a cycle of incarnations together.

However, feeling a connection with someone needn't always be positive – many times we feel drawn to someone who brings negativity or bad experiences into our lives, but that, too, has a purpose. As a Soul you may have been in a similar situation before, very possibly with that soul, and this time you're bound to bring it to a close, to understand that that person or such a person is not serving you and to once and for all withdraw yourself from that scenario.

Why do I write about past lives? I feel that the more you understand where you're coming from, as a Soul, going back even further than this life, the more you are able to understand destructive patterns and transform them, and equally the more able you are to understand that this life is not everything. You will go on after you have left this body. You are now the sum of all your past lives on this planet and in other dimensions. You are unique as a Soul and as a person.

You were created at the same time as all other Souls, we are all equally old, but some of us have spent more lifetimes on Earth than others, therefore feeling more familiar with how this planet works. Some souls may gain great wisdom in a few incarnations, and others may need more time to grow. We all evolve at our own unique pace. As Souls, we will always be, and we have always been. We are eternal beings, forever young, forever growing and learning.

Transforming past-life fears and negative patterns can help you get rid of physical and emotional symptoms you may have developed in this life. This will give you more freedom and happiness.
If you would like to find out more about your past lives, see a past-life regression therapist or immerse yourself in the wonderful books by Dr Brian Weiss.

Nothing in your life is a matter of chance, you chose your family, your sex, your looks, your talents and gifts (some of which you bring over from past lives), your friends and partners, your children, your life path in general, your challenges and opportunities before you incarnate. When writing your chart, you have Counselors by your side who help you, as well as your Spirit Guide, a spirit entity who will be with you throughout this incarnation. They are your advisors, but you make the ultimate decisions on your chart.

You set out to learn and to teach certain things. When your learning and teaching are complete in this life, you return Home. I believe that no Soul will return

Home before their time. Sylvia Browne talks of five "exit points" [11] we chart for ourselves on the Other Side. Each of these exit points is a "way out" back to the Other Side. Which exit point is chosen, is ultimately determined by our Higher Self, and it is always the right moment.

We often hear that we should look after this planet for the sake of our children, as well as out of respect for our ancestors. If you believe in reincarnation, you will know that we actually *are* our ancestors and our children. This planet has seen us before and it may see us again. Let's treat Mother Earth with the love and appreciation we all deserve!

It is extremely likely that you have been on this Earth before.

You are a spiritual being in a human body, having an experience in time and space to perfect your Soul's learning.

This dimension is not your true home, it's only a short trip away from Home.

The person you are now is a sum of all previous incarnations in this dimension and others.

11   Sylvia Browne *Phenomenon*, pp. 115+

❖ Past-life regression and transformation

The aim of past-life regression should always be the transformation of physical and/or emotional pain and hurt.

When a child starts talking about unpleasant memories relating to a past life, it may be enough to explain to them that they are safe now in this new life with their "new" parents. Children tend to move on more quickly than adults because as adults we tend to over-think things. To a child dying in a former life as a fighter pilot in World War II may be a normal part of their existence, as they are still more aware of the Other Side, their True Home where they just came from a little while ago.

To an adult, already rooted in this earthly life, in most cases forgetting about the Other Side completely until this connection is re-awakened, such a memory may be frightening and cause all sorts of emotional and physical conditions.

In April 2012 I discovered a Lourdes candle in my parents' home. My mother did not remember who had given it to her, it looked quite old. She gave it to me and from that moment on I became obsessed with Lourdes. I bought a Lourdes pendant on ebay, put up a figurine of Mother Mary in my house, and started reading about Bernadette Soubirous, studying her life in depth.

In 2008 I had done a past-life regression in Austria where I had re-experienced a lifetime as a nun in 14th century Germany. In that life my childhood was a lonely one, my parents were rich estate owners and never spent any time with me. The only warm and loving person in my life was my nanny, a nun. She played with me and brought a lot of joy into my life. One day, when I was four years old, she broke her vow of chastity behind a bush while I was playing. The shock for me came shortly afterwards – she left with her man. I felt completely abandoned and lonely. A farmer who worked on my parents' estate held me on his arm as I was crying and screaming for her not to go. He tried to comfort me, but I was so hurt and my heart was broken. I felt abandoned and unloved.

The next thing I experienced about that lifetime was me in a convent leading a lonely life as a nun, feeling depressed and hoping every day would be my last. I felt like I was in prison. Looking out of my window, I prayed for God to let me die and end this miserable existence. I experienced no love, no human kindness, no warmth, and no joy during my time in the convent. At the end of this regression, I transformed that energy of loneliness into golden light with a very powerful angel, but for some reason it did not leave me completely. There was still a tiny rest of it in me. Had I gone back for another regression, I could have dissolved the rest of this negative energy, but I went back to England where I had no-one I felt I could trust with my inner secrets.

So when I came across the Lourdes candle in 2012, my past-life memories relating to a life in a convent were triggered again.

As I was reading about Bernadette Soubirous and life in a convent as she had experienced it, I started shaking; I felt as if I could not breathe, I had nightmares. In short, what I was reading would not let me go. It was almost like I was there again, and it was a very unpleasant feeling.

I wanted to travel to Lourdes to transform that energy, I even looked into how much a two-day trip would cost. Clearly, I was serious about it. Luckily my friend Mona happened to be travelling in the French Pyrenees at the time. I asked her to bring me some Lourdes water. I wished that I could go but I was unable to leave my job. I felt I should go to Lourdes to transform the shadows of my past life.

In that same month Madonna released her "Truth or Dare" fragrance. To me the bottle embodied life as a nun in a Catholic convent in the 14th century and I felt fearful just looking at it. Wanting to challenge myself, I ordered a bottle of the perfume. I figured once it would arrive, I would try to get used to it. I did not want it in my house but I decided to face my fear.

In desperation I turned to the angels and asked them to explain to me why those past-life memories affected me so intensely and whether they could help me transform them.

This is what they said to me:

"You have known many a lifetime in France, that ground is very familiar to you. You love France and France has a strong Marian energy in many places. It's the mother-energy of the planet. (...)

Lourdes is a place that leads you to womanhood, to all facets of womanhood. The virgin, the lover, the sister, the mother, the old, the young, the girl, the nun, the powerful woman who faces life on her own, the single mother, the married woman, the mistress, all of it is in the ground at Lourdes and on the site. There is also a strong religious aspect to the site, the worship of Mary, the worship of God, the worship of the worldly priesthood, the Catholic Power Game, the healing and the non-healing, the hope, the agony, the laughter, the sense of community. All of that you find in Lourdes. Our dear Bernadette had an onerous task to do, she did it with dignity, she did it well. Her life was full of challenges, trials and tribulations; her life was that of a true role model. Many people today can identify with some aspect of her life, and she evokes past-life memories in many men and women today who have lived "for God" in previous lives, and who have loved and lost, who have suffered and seen the light at the same time. The dynamics are very complex, the ground is drenched with good and bad and pull and push and evokes transformation. It is transforming you, too, but trust your feelings on how far you want to go at this point. It's not necessary to go all the way, transformation is occurring no matter what. You are fine, you don't need to try to run, just walk, walking is perfect for now. (...) Some swim, some cycle, some run, some walk, some fly, some speed along but in the end only love matters and the path is different for everyone. (...) Everyone is following a different path. (...) No path is better or worse than the other. All souls are equal, all souls are loved, guided and all souls are forever."

This message by the angels had healing properties for me. Since then I have not had bad feelings when I think of convents or nuns, and when the perfume arrived, I felt completely indifferent towards the design of the bottle. I see it every day and use it a lot. The bottle does not trigger a past-life memory for me any more.

The reason I am sharing this story with you is to let you know that past-life memories should and can be transformed, so that we can lead happier, freer lives. What happened to us before this lifetime may affect us but we have the power to get past that and move on. We can decide to accept happiness and fulfill our destiny here and now, regardless of what happened before.

When regressing to a past life, make sure you transform all the energy connected to it.

Only work with someone you trust completely.

If you feel confident enough to regress yourself, the best time is just before you fall asleep. At that time one's mind is most open to the spiritual.

Transforming physical and emotional pain stemming from a past life can have a healing effect on your present situation.

chapter 14

About Death

"Time is life itself, and life resides in the human heart."
(Michael Ende)

"I intend to live forever, or die trying." (Groucho Marx)

"When I think of this being the last time of seeing you
for I do not know how long, I feel it quite impossible to do
anything but love you." (Jane Austen, Mansfield Park)

"Nobody dies. We all live. It is only our human body
that dies." (Lorna Byrne)

* * *

Life is about saying good-bye. Life is a string of "letting-
goes" of events and places, phases in your life (e.g.
childhood, youth), people, possessions, and ultimately
your own body.

Death is yet another good-bye, the ultimate good-bye
for a while, but death is not final. We go on after we die,
we cross over to our true Home, the Other Side. If you

accept life, you have to accept death. Without death, there is no life.

My grandmother Dorothea, when she was dying from cancer, in the last year of her life started to consciously say good-bye to everyone and everything. First, rather than passing on her possessions after her death, she gave away her things. She would say "Would you like to have this mirror? This blouse? This painting?" My grandfather had been a painter, and she had conversations with us all about which paintings we would like and then she would write our names on pieces of paper and stick them at the back of the paintings.

In the last few weeks of her life, she dictated a good-bye letter to me to say good-bye to her best friend in Germany who was an old lady and unable to travel. Relatives would visit to see her, and she would say her goodbyes. She parted with life, little by little. She was brave, humble and grateful for the wonderful people who had surrounded her and were helping her - family, friends and carers. Never did a day pass when she failed to say thank you. By leaving life the way she did, she formed a strong bond with me in her final weeks, promising that "she would be there for us and help us, if there was such a thing".

I have often felt her presence since her death, many times has she sent me inspirational thoughts, I know that she visits to guide and help, and that my happiness is her happiness.

Furthermore, here on Earth those who have died live on in us, through us, through the memories and the inspiration they have given us. Their love and light shines on in our daily actions. You will never forget those who you have loved. Their legacy will continue to motivate you to become a better person and to strive to practise goodness and kindness in honour of their memory.

Death is a temporary good-bye, for we will meet again on the Other Side. When we leave this life, our loved ones who have passed over will be there waiting for us, alongside our Guardian Angel, our angels, spirit guides and beloved animals in spirit. They will welcome us and we will have a big party together, celebrating our reunion.

There is a connection between our dimension and theirs, our true Home. They can send us signs that they are well and they continue to want to see us being happy and fulfilling our dreams.

I have received signs on quite a few occasions from dead relatives who crossed over. One time when I was alone in my house I was woken up in the middle of the night by the sound of a loud bang, just like a perfume bottle had fallen over on my dressing table. But nothing had fallen over! A few minutes later, someone grabbed my big toe. Needless to say, I felt terrified and asked the relative who was causing this to stop. I did not know who it was but I had a feeling it was someone who loved me and just wanted my attention.

A few nights later, I heard a male cough in the middle of the night. The same spirit!
When I went to see a medium a few weeks later, she asked me if I had heard unusual noises in the house. I told her I had and she explained that it had been a deceased male relative of mine, wanting to let me know that he was helping and supporting me!

Have you ever thought of a dead person and suddenly a song comes on the radio that reminds you of them? Have you ever heard unusual noises in your house or have objects been moved? Have you smelt a perfume or after shave that reminded you of a deceased person, even though they were clearly not in the room with you? Have the lights in your house ever gone on or off without you touching the switch? All of those could be signs a crossed over loved one is sending you to tell you they are well and looking after you.

In some rather rare cases, a soul will choose not to go to the Light when they die and to stay in this earthly dimension, scared to let go, believing they will be punished on the Other Side. Such a soul is often referred to as a ghost. "Ghosts" hold on to this dimension, afraid of letting go of their surroundings. In all cases, loving spirit entities will try to convince them, over time, to go into the light and to cross over. This may take several centuries in our understanding of time.

Although I have never seen a ghost with my own eyes, I have lived in a house where things got moved that I knew I had not moved myself and where one of the bathrooms was always particularly cold and I did not like being in there. For instance, I had an angel figurine by one of my windows. The figurine always faced me. One day I returned home and it had turned, facing the window. Yet, nobody had been in the house but myself. I was quite shaken up! Luckily, at the time I knew a clairvoyant who found out that I had an entity in my home who had become attached to me because I reminded him of his dead wife who had died in a car accident. The psychic, with the help of Archangel Michael, persuaded the entity to step into the Light and to go Home. Immediately the atmosphere in my home changed. Living alone, this experience was uncanny to say the least.

If we acknowledge therefore that death is just a temporary good-bye, this means that we will live on after this life. We will continue to exist in another dimension, as we have done before we came here in the first place. This life is just a short trip away from Home. And the Other Side is where we truly belong, where we exist as Souls. As Souls we are permanently in a state of complete happiness and joy on the Other Side, for there we experience themselves in their true state – not restricted by an earthly body but rather assuming a bodily shape, not bound to the laws of time, space, without any physical needs. There we know what it feels like to be creatures of Love and Light, light-ness, beauty, purity, and eternity. We continue to evolve on the Other Side, surrounded with other souls and loving everyone.

As human beings, living a life on this planet, we tend to forget that we are, ultimately, (made of) Love. We are perfect and infinitely beautiful. We are creatures of Light. We tend to forget this because we are limited in this dimension by the laws of time and space and gravity. When we have a human body, we can get ill, we can injure ourselves, we can get hurt emotionally, allow others to control us, and we are prone to physical weakness in many forms. On Earth we can experience darkness, manipulation, coldness, illness, suffering, violence, which can easily lead to us getting tangled up in negativity.

We must not forget that we are spiritual beings living an earthly existence. We must stay grounded whilst acknowledging our divine nature that connects us to one another in eternal love. People who deliberately inflict pain on others, people who are insensitive and suppress others, seeking external power in this world, have forgotten about their loving core.

Above all, it is important to know that no-one can die before they haven't learnt all they came here to learn and taught all they came here to teach. Our Higher Self chooses our final exit point. According to Sylvia Browne[12] we charted five times in our life where we are able to cross over. And we end up taking the one that is in the best interest of our soul's learning. Have you ever been in a life-threatening situation? A car accident perhaps? That may have been one of your exit

---

12 Sylvia Browne *Phenomenon*, pp. 115+

points. Sometimes avoiding an exit point can be a very unspectacular choice of NOT to getting into a car, or on a train on a particular day. So we may avoid an exit point without even realising.

My grandmother told a story of a bombing in Germany when my mother was a baby. During the whole ordeal, she held her new born baby, covering her with her own body, protecting her to the best of her ability. At that moment my grandmother prayed that it was not God's will to take her child's life so soon. I find that remarkable. Instead of praying for her child to live, she directed her prayer at God, whilst acknowledging the fact that God decides on our time of death. Luckily, both were spared that night and lived on to tell the tale.

I feel that it is best not to know the circumstances of our death in advance, as this would greatly affect our happiness and the quality of life.

When I visited the Valley of the Kings in Luxor, Egypt, I was speechless when I saw how spectacular the royal tombs were. I had seen pictures before, but seeing it all with my own eyes, I could not have imagined the sheer beauty of it. I was profoundly touched and wondered – how would it affect your life, how would you live, if you knew that when you die, you will go to such a wonderful place?
Our true Home, the Other Side is obviously not a tomb in Egypt, but try to think of it as a place more beautiful

than you could ever imagine, accompanied by feelings of complete peace and joy.

In some cases, souls choose to leave a legacy behind for many, many generations to come, not only by their lives but also by their deaths. This is true if a person dying from a particular illness or in a certain tragedy that has inspired a charity and raised awareness for certain health issues.

Needless to say, the founders of all the major religions have left an enormous legacy behind.

Sometimes, in the case of Pompeii or the Titanic, history has remained "frozen in time", inspiring many people to this day to reflect on life and death.

The thought that unexpected tragedy may strike at any moment makes us appreciate life and our loved ones even more. Furthermore, our last deed may be a heroic one, one that we may be remembered for for centuries. Would you have died a hero on the Titanic? Would you have given up your seat in a lifeboat for a woman or a child?

We do not know when our time is up. Therefore, I believe, we must never part in anger and we must live life with kindness to the best of our ability, so that we are ready to go at any time without regrets. The moment itself and its circumstances are a mystery, as this quote shows:

"I never saw a wreck, and I have never been wrecked, nor was I ever in any predicament that threatened to end in disaster of any sort." (Captain Smith, Commander of the Titanic, in an interview in 1907[13])

Death is not final.

Love lives on in us, and memories of loved ones can inspire and motivate us to grow every single day.

There will be a reunion with crossed-over loved ones at our moment of death. We will be together again on the Other Side, our true Home.

Loved ones who have passed over continue to watch over us with great love, in some cases even asking for our forgiveness for pain and suffering caused by them during their lifetime.

Loved ones who have crossed over may give us signs that they are well.

We are spiritual beings of Love and Light.

This life is only temporary.

---

13 Anne Marie Welsh *Heroes of the Titanic*, p. 10

chapter 15

About Food

"If more of us valued food and cheer and song above hoarded gold, it would be a merrier world."
(J.R.R. Tolkien)

"All you need is love. But a little chocolate now and then doesn't hurt." (Charles M. Schulz)

"Seize the moment. Remember all those women on the 'Titanic' who waved off the dessert cart."
(Erma Bombeck)

* * *

"I really shouldn't ..."

"Go on, have some chocolate!"

"Oh no, I shouldn't ..."

When it comes to food, don't be foolish! If you are suffering from an illness that forbids you to eat certain things, i.e. your body has decided to reject certain foods, then stay away from those foods. Live a healthy life to the best of your ability, but also enjoy your food at the same time. Treat your body with respect, eat lots of fresh fruit and vegetables, don't eat microwave dinners!

My skin improved dramatically when I finally stopped eating microwave food and started to cook for myself. In doing that, I took time for myself to create something good for me, putting my own (loving) energy into the food as I am making it.

If you have a busy week, cook at the weekend and freeze some food for the week ahead. If you can, take turns cooking with your partner/older children.

Since 2007, when I was at a Doreen Virtue seminar in London, I have not eaten any meat or chocolate. I had been thinking about giving up those two things for a while. As for meat, I no longer wanted to eat dead flesh. As regards chocolate, my chocolate addiction was getting out of hand – I simply ate too much and was unable to cut down. When Doreen asked the audience to give up eating something that we felt we did not want to eat any more, I focused on meat and chocolate. It worked for me. I feel much healthier and "lighter" not eating meat any more, and when I look at chocolate today my mouth does not even water. I am completely indifferent to it.

I encourage everyone to look at their eating habits and to make the necessary changes for a healthier body. You will know best which foods to leave out or cut back on.

At the same time, I do not like it when people eat a dessert and afterwards "feel guilty" about eating it. That is simply stupid to me! You have to be able to enjoy your food, too, and occasionally eat something you do not eat on a daily basis, and your body won't hold it against you. The reason such behaviour annoys me is this story:

A few weeks before my grandmother Dorothea died from cancer in 1994 I made spaghetti. I remember her eating every bite of her pre-cut pasta with extreme joy, commenting on how lovely it tasted and how well I had cooked it. She absolutely loved my spaghetti! It was wonderful to see her enjoy her food, especially as she was becoming weaker and weaker every day. Unfortunately, less than an hour afterwards, she was sick, bringing up the meal as well as vomiting blood. It was heartbreaking to see this. From that moment on, I made a promise to myself that I was always going to be grateful if I could eat "normally".

Being able to digest food normally should not be taken for granted, so enjoy your food and be grateful!

Look after your body.

Be kind to your body.

Remember it was you who chose your body before you incarnated.

Enjoy your food and be grateful.

Do the cooking yourself; eat fresh as much as possible.

If you have a particular health problem, do not take any risks and follow your prescribed regime.

❖ A note on alcohol

Generally speaking, substances that compromise your ability to keep a clear mind are not to be advised, especially if you are trying to open up to the spirit world for the first time. For clear communication with the angels and in order to channel their messages accurately, we need to be grounded and focused. Respect your body all the time, and you will feel much happier and healthier.

Alcohol and other drugs compromise your ability to think clearly, and they can have a harmful effect on the body.

To communicate with the angels and to channel their messages you need a clear head.

chapter 16

             — ❦ —

About Nature

"Come forth into the light of things. Let nature be your teacher." (William Wordsworth)

"Flowers are the alphabet of angels, whereby they write on the fields and hills mysterious truths."
(Benjamin Franklin)

"And I can hear the brook laughing all the way up here. Have you ever noticed what cheerful things brooks are? They're always laughing. Even in winter-time I've heard them under the ice."
(L.M. Montgomery, Anne of Green Gables)

* * *

What is your favourite type of landscape? What view makes your heart sing? Do you prefer hills, mountains, rivers, lakes, forests, fields, the desert or the seaside? Which season is your favourite? How does nature look most beautiful to you? In lush shades of green in the summer or covered in snow and ice in the winter?

Do you like outdoor sports? Which ones and where do you go to play them?

Can you name your number-one flower or tree?

What nature sounds do you like? Rain, thunder, ocean waves, crickets, birdsong?

What smells in nature are you particularly fond of? What is the smell of summer/autumn/winter/spring?

If you have ever visited a lavender field in the summer, for example, you will know the intense effect that scents and colour can have on your mood and well-being. What an amazing experience that was for me when I went to the Cotswold Lavender Farm[14]!

What memories do you have related to nature? Did you roll down hills as a child? Did you collect chestnuts in the autumn? When was the last time you built a snowman or had a snowball fight? When did you last feel the warm grass or hot sand underneath your feet? Was it a pleasant sensation for you?

The first time I ever laid eyes on the Mediterranean Sea my heart skipped a beat! How fabulously beautiful the waves were as they were dashing onto the rocks. The sound, the smell, the look of the ocean! Ever-changing, yet harmonious and calming! I will never forget it.

The aspect that nature adds to our lives by its beauty must be valued highly: The variety of colours, smells, as

---

14 www.cotswoldlavender.co.uk

well as the infinite possibility of adventure, discovery, fun, joy, and laughter. Nature is there for us, no matter who we are or what our circumstances in life may be. Nature never judges us, it is just there to love us and lift us up.

Needless to say, we need the elements that nature/ Mother Earth/ this planet provides for us. We need air to breathe, water to drink, fire to stay warm, and earth to grow food. We need the rain, the sun, the light, the darkness.

Like we find in nature, we have a life cycle of our own. When we die, our bodies will become part of the very ground we walk on. Thus, we are part of this Earth, part of this planet and we must take responsibility for it! Our planet is facing major environmental issues like ocean acidification, pollution, ozone layer depletion, deforestation, and over-fishing, just to name a few.

We need to respect the environment by thinking "green" in some way at least, be it only by recycling and buying environmentally friendly products and foods. We must do our bit in order to preserve this planet for many generations to come.

Another aspect of nature is that it is a great healer. Just think of the healing properties of certain plants, trees, as well as crystals, minerals and vitamins. Medicine can prove the effectiveness of those on a scientific level, whereas the spiritual element, the energy aspect, is equally important. There are many energy sprays and essences available that reflect and capture nature energies to support healing processes on a physical, mental, emotional and/or spiritual level. Such remedies can bring to light emotional, mental, physical and/or spiritual issues and help us accept and heal them by activating our own self-healing abilities. We can also meditate with nature energies (trees, plants, landscapes), which can be an infinitely beautiful (healing) experience.

In addition, as discussed in *About Spirit Helpers*, fairies and other nature spirits teach us not to take ourselves too seriously. They want us to be who we are and to enjoy life whilst respecting and loving the environment as well as each other, and they are willing to help us with anything, if we only ask.

Working with tree and nature energies in the form of meditation and channeling, as well as using the "Triangel" essences and symbols developed by Austrian therapist Angela Dlabaja[15] has helped me enormously to grow as a person. I am much more aware of myself as well as the world around me and I have become more appreciative of nature. There are many types of flower/tree/nature essences available, e.g. Bach flower remedies and Australian bush flower essences. These contain the energy of the tree or plant in question, which directly affects all levels of our energy field. My personal favourite nature remedies

---

15 www.triangel-naturelixiere.net

are the Triangel Nature Essences mentioned before which I use on a daily basis.

If you need healing, comforting, nurturing, stress-release, strength, guidance or want to deal with emotional, psychological, spiritual or mental issues in your life, why not turn to nature for help? You can simply go for a walk or close your eyes for a few moments, imagining a beautiful landscape. Get a new perspective, inhale and exhale and consciously acknowledge the beauty you feel, see and hear.

Nature is our ever-loving, ever-changing, beautiful companion, healer and teacher.

Take a walk to reload your batteries and gain a different perspective.

Meditate with nature energies and/or use nature essences of your choice to support physical, mental, emotional or spiritual healing in your life.

Allow yourself to experience life the fairy way – focus on the fun element!

❖ About the weather

"In the spring, I have counted 136 different kinds of weather inside of 24 hours." (Mark Twain)

"It is only in sorrow bad weather masters us; in joy we face the storm and defy it." (Amelia Barr)

"A change in the weather is sufficient to recreate the world and ourselves." (Marcel Proust)

* * *

I believe that the weather has an effect on one's wellbeing. As Light Therapy suggests, we need sunshine to keep our spirits up, as well as for certain physiological conditions. Sunlight also gives us Vitamin D which is essential for bone health and to support the immune system.

Bad (rainy) weather, which we see a lot of here in the UK, can make you feel frustrated and depressed. If all you see all day are grey skies and pouring rain, accompanied by howling winds, this may dampen your mood. I have always found that windy conditions in particular can give me a headache.

If the weather is bad, you have two choices: persevere in the rain or stay inside. For me, the second choice works best. If the weather is bad at a weekend, I try and find things to do that I enjoy inside, e.g. I might cook something, read, watch TV, paint or do other things to make me feel more cheerful.

You could even invite friends round, and, if you have children, find fun things to do with them in the house, e.g. play board games. Alternatively, you could dress in raingear and play outside. Your children may even prefer that version.

We are unable to influence the weather, but we can deal with it in such a way that it brings us happiness rather than frustration.

Lorna Byrne suggests that we can ask the angels to influence the weather[16], and to bring us more sunshine! Why not try it? I'd certainly like more sunshine, angels! Thank you!

Enjoy the sunshine while it lasts.

If you are emotionally affected by bad weather, try to cheer yourself up.

---

16   Lorna Byrne in an interview in July 2012

chapter 17

About Pets

"Until one has loved an animal, a part of one's soul remains unawakened." (Anatole France)

* * *

I believe that we are reunited with our beloved pets when we get to the Other Side. I also believe that dogs, cats and possibly other pets/animals can reincarnate to be with us. However, they do not have a chart, as there is no learning attached to their being here, their souls do not progress as ours do.[17] The relationship between a pet and its owner ideally is a loving one, and both benefit from it.

Having a pet brings with it a big commitment. Unfortunately, living on my own, travelling to Austria around three times a year, and working full-time, I am unable to have a pet at present. Oh how I'd love to have a dog! I can't wait to one day have one, it is a big

---

17   Sylvia Browne *All Pets go to Heaven*, p. 4

dream and a deep wish of mine and has been for as long as I can remember.

As children my brother and I were allowed a guinea-pig which we named Martin. Martin was a reasonably lively but also very timid animal and I have to admit that the work involved in keeping him was mainly done by my parents. We also had a huge cage full of budgies in various colours, some yellow, some green, some blue. They were not tame, though very beautiful and entertaining.

The wish for a cuddly pet, a dog preferably, a cute, reliable and loving companion, has been with me for as long as I can remember. I hope that one day my wish will come true.

Pets are our loving and faithful companions not just in this dimension, but also on the Other Side.

chapter 18

❧

About Affirmations and Prayer

Affirmations can help to heal emotional, psychological, mental and physical wounds.

For me, affirmations are prayers directed at oneself, as well as God, full of love and hope.

In one house where I lived I decorated an entire wall in my bedroom with little cards on which I had written positive words like LIGHT, LOVE, COMPASSION, COURAGE, GRATITUDE, ASSERTION, REINVENTION, HONESTY, WISDOM, SECURITY, PASSION, DIVINE SELF, CHANGE, CONFIDENCE, SPONTANEITY, CLARITY, INDIVIDUALITY, and many more. Every day I looked at it, even though my life at the time was a struggle. I believe that surrounding myself with positive words and thoughts helped me keep my faith whilst going through a difficult time.

Choose some of these affirmations to say a few times a day or to put up around the house.

You may also wish to write your own. Make sure they are worded in a positive way.

- I have love in my life.

- I have beauty in my life.

- I have possibilities in my life.

- I have joy in my life.

- I have strength in my Soul.

- I have excitement in my life.

- I feel free and abundant.

- I do the work of God with glory.

- I love myself in all my incarnations through time and space.

- I love.

- I shine with confidence.

- I am the sunlight on Earth.

- I speak my truth.

- I see light and clarity.

- I know my Soul is pure.

- I am loved, protected and guided.

- I see the truth.

- I know that I am a Child of God.

SACRED PRAYER

I ask you, dear angels, to let me feel joy in my life.

Give me the strength and courage to
claim my place in this world.

Lead me to the people and places that will help me
to live my dreams and fulfill my heart's desire.

Let me feel the love and guidance that
is with me every minute of my life.

Create miracles for me and my loved ones.

Heal my body and my heart where healing is needed.

Thank you, dear angels.

Today I will ...

Make a promise to myself

Listen

Hold the door for someone

Put love into everything I do

Shine my light

Give a present for no reason

Do something for the environment

Start a new hobby

Practise patience

Tell a loved one I love them

Trust God

Allow myself to feel complete

Make someone laugh

Forgive

Accept a helping hand

Do a kind deed

Feel grateful

Talk to my Guardian Angel

Cook with fresh ingredients

Acknowledge my spirit helpers

Spend time alone

Eat something special

Share my lunch

Say a prayer

Tell myself I'm beautiful

Pay a compliment to someone

Visualize success

Look after my inner and outer beauty

Invite someone over

Ring a friend

Smile at someone

Go out of my way to do something nice for someone

...

What will you do today?

Guided Meditation to Connect with Your Spirit Helpers

Record yourself reading these lines. Use the recording to do the meditation or work with a friend reading this to you. Pause in the indicated places. You may choose to play soothing music in the background.

Close your eyes. Feel where you're sitting and the position of your body, your hands and arms. Notice your breathing. Breathe in and out. ... As you exhale, you feel all the tension inside your body leaving your body. Feel your shoulders relax, your arms and feet relax. Any worries, or hurt you might feel drift away and become unimportant. As you inhale, imagine bright white light entering your body from the top of your head. The white light fills your body, all your organs, your aura, the room you are in, the house you are in, the town, the country and the globe. ...

There is white sparkling bright light everywhere. Shift your attention to your feet. Feel your feet touching the ground. Let the white light leave your body through your feet. Feel your feet firmly on the ground. Place them on the ground, feel the connection with Mother Earth. Your feet give your body perfect balance; you are safe and well grounded at this moment. Your whole body is perfectly relaxed and you feel at ease. ...

Now visualise yourself in a beautiful meadow. Can you smell the fragrance of the flowers? Maybe you can feel the sun on your skin. Listen! What do you hear? ...

Take a step forward. There are colourful birds everywhere, singing beautifully and greeting you. You lift your hands up to the sky and greet the clouds that are drifting past. The sky is light blue and you feel calm and happy just looking up at it. In the middle of the meadow there is a tree. ...

Walk to that tree. What does it look like? Is it an old or a young tree? What is its shape? Has it got leaves? If it does, what colour are they? What does the trunk look like? Do you feel small or tall next to the tree? ...

All your worries, insecurities, and doubts are in your rucksack. Now put down your rucksack and leave it next to the tree. Ask the tree to look after it for you. You put it down by the tree. Immediately you feel calmer and lighter and relieved. You step back into the meadow.

The bees are buzzing around you and there are birds in the sky above you. You see butterflies, merrily dancing from flower to flower. Suddenly you feel a strong, yet warm breeze in your hair and face. ...

You turn around and in the distance you see a figure coming towards you. Who is it? Is it an angel? Is it an animal? Is it a person? Someone you know? What does the being look like? What are they doing? Are they speaking to you? Take some time to enjoy their company... You can ask them a question if you want ...

Feel their loving energy warming your heart ...

Sit down or lie down on the grass with your guide. Enjoy the peace and serenity that surrounds you. Hear the sound of nature ...

Your guide asks you to give them any doubt, fear, or pain you have to take to Heaven and transform so that it either goes away or becomes small enough for you to handle. ...

Your spirit is starting to retreat but before they go they give you a present. What is it? What colour is it? You feel your helper's loving energy around you, wrapping around you like a blanket and making you feel quite cosy. Your heart feels warm and light and you smile at your guide. Say thank you for the present.

Say goodbye and thank you to your guide. They give you a hug and then gently wave good-bye to you as you are walking back to the tree. You see your rucksack by the tree but its appearance has changed. What does it look like now? Take the rucksack or what's left of it, and thank the tree for looking after it.

Say good-bye to the meadow and take a few deep breaths. When you are ready, become aware of your body, your surroundings and open your eyes. You are here again.

How do you feel now?

FOREVER YOU in a Nutshell

In the face of eternity we are forever - forever evolving, forever learning, forever young!

I believe that if I can be happy at this moment, I can be happy at any moment. I cannot ever be happy if I cannot be happy right now, as the now of tomorrow is nothing but another moment in time.

I believe in kindness.

I believe that all Souls are, at their core, pure, light-ful, and loving, no matter what manifestations we may see on this planet.

I believe that we can change our fate for the better whilst respecting our own destiny.

I believe that all souls are equal before God.

I believe that nobody can die before their time, and each death bears meaning to those left behind and holds an opportunity to grow and to gain depth.

I believe in eternal life.

I believe that love, true love, is the only real emotion, and there are reasons why people have complex issues tied to what they perceive as "love". What we call love, is sometimes an accumulation of fear, anger, selfishness and (self-) destruction.

I believe that we need to focus on the good and the positive.

I believe that suffering can bring great transformation and growth.

I believe in a balance of give and take in all loving and successful relationships.

I believe in sharing.

I believe all children should be loved and told they are beautiful.

I believe in self-love and self-acceptance, not self-flagellation and abuse of one's own soul.

I believe in taking responsibility for one's actions.

I believe in treating this planet with respect.

I believe in giving. Give, give, give, and if in doubt, give more. Tokens of appreciation may open doors, or they may open hearts.

I believe we should learn to forgive and forget. It is hard to move away from disappointment, but we learn from it. And part of that learning is to make sure it doesn't happen again.

I believe in trusting one's gut instinct, one's inner voice, no matter what.

I believe in deliverance and mercy.

I believe in beauty.

I believe in me.

Acknowledgements

I would like to thank all those people who have made my life as Marii possible. Not just those two people who brought me into the world, or even the person who gave birth to me, all of you, who, through the years have encouraged me to move forward, to stick to my dream, to be patient and to learn along the way. I would like to thank all of you who have been there in the good times and the bad, and who have never given up on me. You made my life worth living when I felt I had nothing to live for.

Thus I'd like to thank my parents Angelika and Herbert, my brother Christian, my grandparents Dorothea, Ernst, Steffi and Franz, as well as my best friend Magdalena. Thank you for always being there for me.

Equally, I would like to thank all those who made my life difficult, miserable at times, who made me feel like I was not good enough, who have lied to me and abandoned me when I needed them the most, who made false promises to me when I needed to belong. Without you, I would not be the person I am today, and I would not have developed the spiritual beliefs I hold now.

Thank you my dear spirit guides, angels and other helpers on the Other Side, for you have stood by me and loved me no matter what.

Thank you all Souls who have known me in any lifetime on Earth or in any other dimension. I know I am the sum of all my pasts, the master of my present and the queen of my future, forever learning, forever loving and forever young, as are you who are reading this.

Mahalo. Malama pono.

Acknowledgements (continued)

Very special thanks to Magdalena Heinich for editing *Forever You* for me with great love and dedication in the first instance.

Furthermore, I would like to thank the following people from the bottom of my heart:

Angelika Zierhut, Herbert Zierhut, Christian Zierhut, Regine Gabler-Anderl, Maria "Puki" Anderl, Thomas Gabler, Ghader Rassoulian, Johannes Anderl, Dorothea and Ernst Anderl, Steffi and Franz Zierhut, Fritz Zierhut, Margarete Landgraf, Beate Schaffer, Helga Weber, Romana Dolleisch, Angela Dlabaja, Janet Higginbotham, Grit Lexa, Latife Strong, Caroline Richings, Andrea Grünauer, Shelby Owen, Stephanie Cornthwaite, Keelyn Walsh and everyone at Balboa Press.